AMERICAN EPIC

★ ★ ★ ★ ★ ★ ★ ★

The Companion Book to **THE PBS SERIES**

T BONE BURNETT
ROBERT REDFORD
JACK WHITE

present

AMERICAN

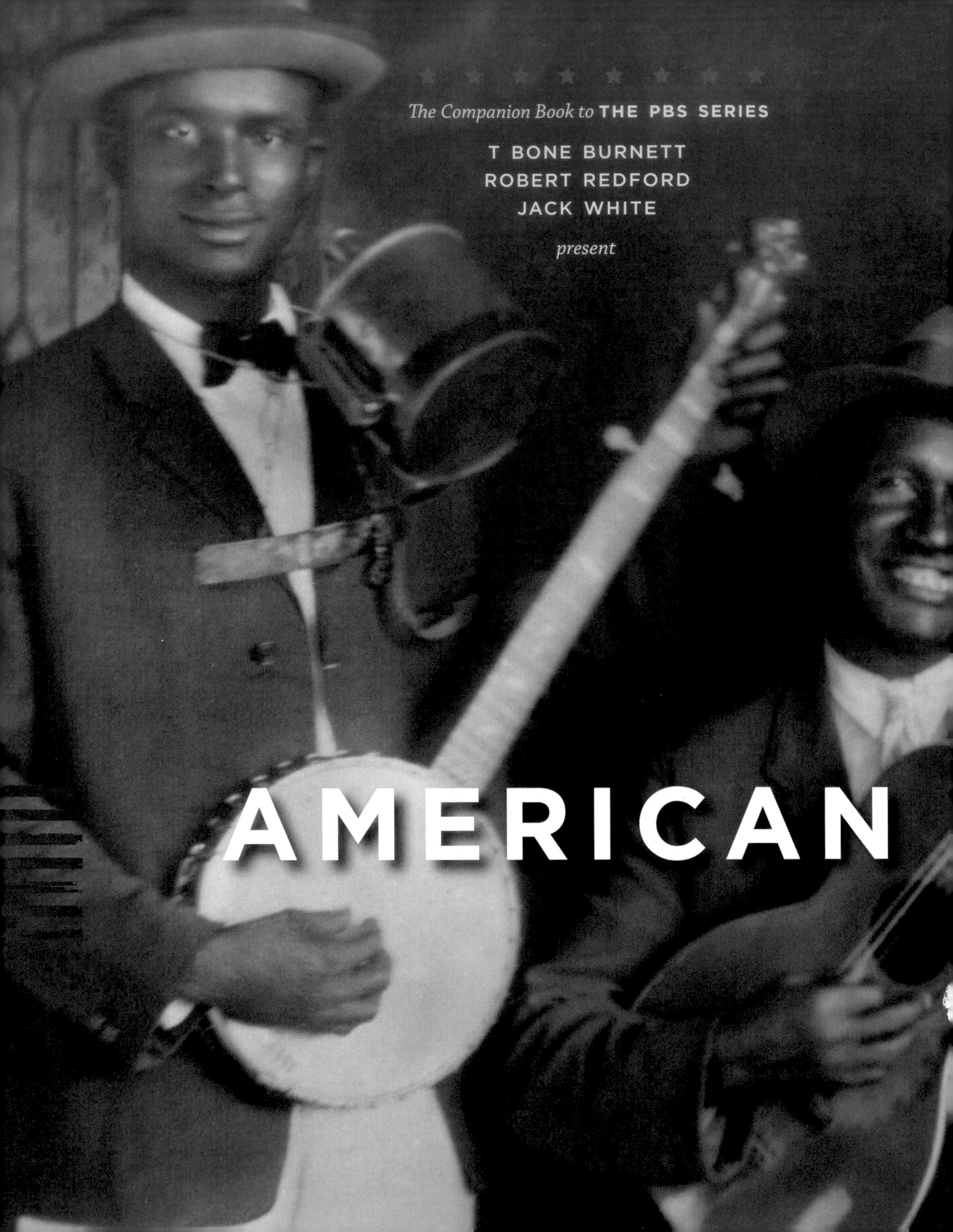

EPIC
WHEN MUSIC GAVE AMERICA HER VOICE

BERNARD MAcMAHON & ALLISON McGOURTY
WITH ELIJAH WALD

TOUCHSTONE

New York London Toronto Sydney New Delhi

Previous page: *Cannon's Jug Stompers* (from left to right):
Gus Cannon, Ashley Thompson, and Noah Lewis

Touchstone
An Imprint of Simon & Schuster, Inc.
1230 Avenue of the Americas
New York, NY 10020

First Touchstone hardcover edition May 2017

TOUCHSTONE and colophon are registered trademarks of Simon & Schuster, Inc.

For information about special discounts for bulk purchases, please
contact Simon & Schuster Special Sales at 1-866-506-1949 or
business@simonandschuster.com.

The Simon & Schuster Speakers Bureau can bring authors to your live event. For
more information or to book an event, contact the Simon & Schuster Speakers
Bureau at 1-866-248-3049 or visit our website at www.simonspeakers.com.

Interior design by Lorie Pagnozzi

Manufactured in the United States of America

10 9 8 7 6 5 4 3 2 1

Library of Congress Cataloging-in-Publication Data

Names: MacMahon, Bernard, 1970– author. | McGourty, Allison, author. | Wald,
    Elijah, author.
Title: American epic : when music gave America her voice / by Bernard
    MacMahon and Allison McGourty with Elijah Wald.
Description: New York : Touchstone, 2017. | Includes bibliographical
    references.
Identifiers: LCCN 2016001493| ISBN 9781501135606 (hardcover) | ISBN
    9781501135613 (pbk.)
Subjects: LCSH: Sound recording industry—United States—History. | Popular
    music—United States—History and criticism. | Popular culture—United
    States—History—20th century.
Classification: LCC ML3790 .M15 2016 | DDC 781.640973/09042—dc23 LC
record available at http://lccn.loc.gov/2016001493

ISBN 978-1-5011-3560-6
ISBN 978-1-5011-3562-0 (ebook)

TO DUKE ERIKSON, WITHOUT WHOM *AMERICAN EPIC* WOULD NOT EXIST

CONTENTS

TITLE	ENVELOPE NUMBER	
INTRODUCTION		
THE FIRST TIME AMERICA HEARD HERSELF	1	
I'LL GET A BREAK SOMEDAY:	2	
IN THE SHADOW OF CLINCH MOUNTAIN:	3	
MY HEART KEEPS SINGING:	4	
GONNA DIE WITH MY HAMMER IN MY HAND:	5	
DOWN THE DIRT ROAD:	6	
CHANT OF THE SNAKE DANCE:	7	
BIRD OF PARADISE:	8	
MAL HOMBRE:	9	
ALLONS À LAFAYETTE:	10	
AVALON BLUES:	11	
THE AMERICAN EPIC SESSIONS	12	
TRAVEL AND THE CREW		
ACKNOWLEDGMENTS		
SOURCES		
PHOTO CREDITS		

RECORD NUMBER	ARTIST
1	
9	
WILL SHADE AND THE MEMPHIS JUG BAND 31	
THE CARTER FAMILY 57	
ELDER J. E. BURCH 79	
DICK JUSTICE AND THE WILLIAMSON BROTHERS 101	
CHARLEY PATTON AND THE MISSISSIPPI DELTA BLUES 117	
THE HOPI INDIAN CHANTERS 131	
JOSEPH KEKUKU 151	
LYDIA MENDOZA 169	
THE BREAUX FAMILY 189	
MISSISSIPPI JOHN HURT 215	
233	
264	
271	
275	
279	

MADE IN U. S. A.

★ ★ ★ ★ INTRODUCTION ★ ★

TEN YEARS AGO, WE SET OUT ON A JOURNEY TO EXPLORE THE VAST RANGE OF ETHNIC, RURAL, AND REGIONAL MUSIC RECORDED IN THE UNITED STATES DURING THE LATE 1920S. THAT WAS AN AMAZING PERIOD—THE FIRST TIME AMERICANS HEARD EACH OTHER IN ALL THEIR RICHNESS AND VARIETY—AND IT RESHAPED THE WHOLE CONCEPT OF POPULAR MUSIC. ALMOST A CENTURY LATER, WE WANTED TO SEE IF WE COULD STILL EXPERIENCE THAT MUSIC DIRECTLY, AMONG THE PEOPLE WHO MADE IT, IN THE PLACES IT WAS PLAYED, FEELING THE THRILL OF THE MOMENT WHEN IT WAS CAPTURED ON RECORDS.

WE STARTED BY CHOOSING SOME ARTISTS AND RECORDINGS THAT WE FOUND PARTICULARLY MOVING, THEN SET OUT TO TRACE THEM THROUGH SPACE AND TIME. AT TIMES IT SEEMED A QUIXOTIC QUEST, BUT AS WE TRAVELED, WE KEPT BEING STARTLED BY THE OVERLAPS OF OLD AND NEW, THE WAYS IN WHICH THE MUSIC OF THE PAST CONTINUED TO RESONATE AND REFLECT THE PRESENT. WE HAD LEFT OUR HOME IN TWENTY-FIRST-CENTURY BRITAIN TO TRAVEL ACROSS A FOREIGN COUNTRY AND DEEP INTO THE PAST, BUT OVER AND OVER AGAIN, THE PEOPLE WE MET AND THE PLACES WE VISITED FELT VERY FAMILIAR AND VERY MUCH IN THE PRESENT.

Bernard MacMahon

New York

The film crew

Louisiana

"WE WANTED TO PRESERVE THE WORDS OF THE PEOPLE WE MET AND GIVE
READERS A CHANCE TO VISIT WITH THEM AND HEAR THEIR STORIES . . ."

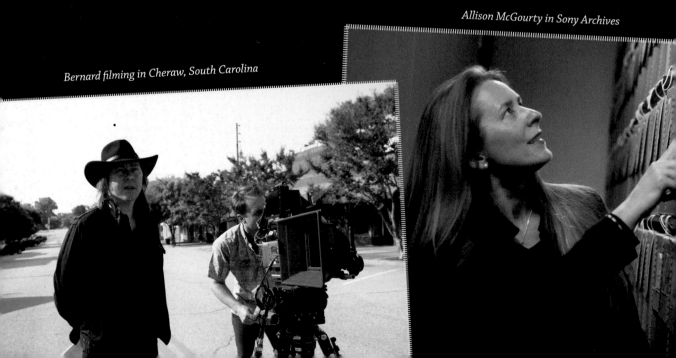

Allison McGourty in Sony Archives

Bernard filming in Cheraw, South Carolina

That journey became the *American Epic* project: a series of films, a series of albums, and this book. We wanted to preserve the words of the people we met and give readers a chance to visit with them and hear their stories, and to share the hundreds of photographs, advertisements, postcards, and other material we found along the way.

As we traveled, we were always conscious of following well-beaten paths: we were retracing the commercial expeditions of the record company scouts who fanned out across America in the 1920s in search of new styles of music, and also the voyages of the many musicians who left homes and loved ones in hopes of having their voices and instruments preserved on fragile shellac discs. We wanted to bring those experiences to life: to escape the museum atmosphere of history books and reissue albums by going to the places where the musicians lived and the recordings were made, walking the streets and breathing the air these people breathed, meeting their families, and immersing ourselves in their worlds.

We prepared ourselves by reading the histories, combing the archives, and talking with the experts, and also went on a technological journey that involved re-creating a studio of the period, with a 1920s-era Western Electric amplifier and weight-driven Scully lathe to do our own recording sessions. We were seeking simultaneously to understand how music was created and preserved in the past and to experience that music as directly as possible in the present. We first fell in love with the rural and ethnic recordings of the 1920s because they touched and moved us as modern listeners, and we wanted to extend and explore that direct emotional connection.

There is a unique freshness and vitality to those early recordings, made by people who in many cases had never imagined they would be heard or appreciated beyond their own communities. That first, experimental period was dauntingly brief: the Depression hit in 1929, and record companies went out of business or fell back on reliable sales formulas. But for a few years they were taking chances and recorded an astonishing range of styles, and those recordings forever changed the scope and meaning of popular music: instead of urban theater, concert, and cabaret performers singing the compositions of professional composers and lyricists, they captured the voices, rhythms, and melodies of regular working people, the music that evolved into country and western, rhythm and blues, and beyond—rock 'n' roll, funk, punk, rap, tejano, reggae, and myriad other styles around the world.

We have spent our whole lives surrounded by those later styles, and when we discovered these first, formative records, we were startled to find that many of them—the ones that matter to us—were every bit as thrilling and relevant as the newer records we also loved. Their age added a level of mystery, an exotic frisson: they seemed to come from somewhere different and magical, and we spun fantasies of the times, places, and people connected to those sounds.

Over the years, those records became close friends, accompanying us as we grew and changed, through all our hopes, fears, joys, and sorrows. *American Epic* was a chance to travel home with them, to see where they came from and meet their families and neighbors. It was a way of bringing them closer, giving them new life, understanding them better, and knowing them more deeply.

That process wasn't all sunshine and smiles—we traveled to beautiful places and met some of the most wonderful people we

have ever known, but we also heard stories of poverty and discrimination, of hard times and troubled lives. The power of the music comes in a large part from its role as a comfort and release for people trapped in difficult situations. But the journey was always rewarding, not despite but because of those connections. As we traveled, the songs became less and less connected to old discs and vanished eras, and more and more to living people and communities.

We first heard this music thousands of miles from its birthplace and across an ocean. Growing up in Scotland and London, we had romantic notions of America, a place seen in films and on television, with cowboys and Indians, sweeping prairies and towering skyscrapers. American music was part of that, but also apart from it, especially when we listened to older artists like the Carter Family, the Memphis Jug Band, Mississippi John Hurt, and Lydia Mendoza. They spoke to us with a directness that seemed more human and intimate, and more earthy and real than the cinematic fantasies.

We set out to explore why particular recordings gave us particular feelings and touched particular emotions, and found that an important part of that was the way they reflected particular communities, and the particular geography of the places where those people lived. The more we traveled, the more we became convinced that sounds and styles arise from specific environments, and you can only truly un-

The Triumph Church choir

Bernard directing the Triumph Church shoot

derstand them when you go where they came from. Of course, you can enjoy music without hearing it in its native setting, but we kept finding that we had never fully experienced a recording or felt it to the depth of our souls until we listened to it in its home.

We eventually coined the term "geographonics" to express that idea: that some sounds seem to trace the contours and take their flavor from the soil of specific places. From the hills of West Virginia to the streets of Memphis, the deserts of Arizona, the Louisiana bayous, or the beaches of Hawai'i, the rhythms and melodies are inextricably entwined with the landscape and echo the sounds of the wind and waves, the birds and crickets, the trains and traffic.

That is the unique magic of the recordings that set us on this journey: before the 1920s,

virtually all recorded music came from a world of professional performance, intentionally designed to be acceptable to a mass audience. From the majesty of Beethoven to the buffoonery of the minstrel ditties, and from sentimental parlor ballads to the jerky rhythms of ragtime, records were intended to appeal to universal tastes and reach the broadest possible range of listeners.

With the arrival of radio, many of those listeners had a simpler, cheaper way of hearing those mass-market styles. Records were expensive for a lot of people, and each disc could hold only three or four minutes of music on either side. Radio provided urban listeners with everything from symphony concerts to the latest hits, in a constant stream of music, and cost nothing beyond the purchase price of the basic set. By the mid-1920s, record sales were plummeting, and record companies responded by seeking out new markets: regional and ethnic groups whose favored styles were not being broadcast, and rural listeners who had no electricity but could listen to records on windup phonographs. At the same time, the new technology of electrical recording made it possible to record a much wider range of sounds and to send portable field units around the country rather than bringing all the artists to centers like New York and Chicago.

The result was that, for the first time, a vast range of rural and working-class Americans were recorded, could hear people who sounded like them on records, and became aware of one another's music. Record company scouts and producers acted to some extent as gatekeepers, but in those first years they were largely groping in the dark and willing to take a chance on almost anything that was interesting and different. When Ralph Peer recorded Fiddlin' John Carson during a trip to Atlanta in 1923, it was only because a local store owner had promised to buy the entire initial pressing—Peer thought Carson's initial recording sounded terrible, and was astounded when the store owner called him a week later, shouting, "This is a riot! I gotta get ten thousand records down here right now!"

Peer is recalled as a pioneer and visionary, and his experience with Carson is often framed as the eureka moment of the rural recording boom. But the next chapter tends to be left out of that story: as Carson's records took off across the South, Peer began to get letters from other rural musicians who thought they should also be recorded, and when he failed to respond promptly, a harmonica player named Henry Whitter made the trek from southern Virginia to his New York office. Both Carson and Whitter made dozens of records in the next few years, and as other scouts headed out into the hinterlands and thousands of other rural artists were preserved on discs, the journeys were always in both directions.

As we traveled across America, we often felt like we were retracing the paths of the old record scouts, but we were also consciously following the trails of the artists themselves: the Carter Family traveling to Texas for a radio career, the Hopi Indian Chanters bringing their ancient ceremonies to New York and Washington, and Joseph Kekuku leaving Hawai'i for the mainland, London, and the capitals of Europe. Looking back from the twenty-first century, it is easy to think of those early recordings as historical curiosities, but the people who made them were modern human beings, recording with modern technologies and having modern experiences, and that is one of the reasons their music still speaks to us so directly. Romantic as it may be to think of Mississippi John Hurt as a poor sharecropper living in the remote Delta hamlet of Avalon, he was also someone who traveled to New York in December 1928 for a pair of recording sessions, blazing the trail he would follow thirty-five years later to make a sensational appearance at the Newport Folk Festival.

Along with our geographical journeys, we also made a technological journey, and it was likewise an attempt both to understand the past and to make it live in the present. With the engineer and audio archaeologist Nick Bergh, we rebuilt a 1920s recording studio, and one of the most exciting parts of our project was reliving the experience of recording direct to discs, with one microphone and a weight-driven lathe. It was a loving exercise in historical re-creation—but the artists we recorded included not only revivalist musicians like Jerron Paxton and Pokey LaFarge and rural icons like Willie Nelson and Merle Haggard, but also modern, urban stars like Jack White, Nas, Alabama Shakes, and Elton John. It was another way to bring past and present together, and the experience of recording with that equipment gave us new insights into the ways it captured and transformed sound—which in turn allowed us to hear the old records with new ears, and to produce albums of our favorite 1920s recordings that took advantage of our new knowledge, bringing out subtle vocal inflections, instrumental textures, and even the sound of the rooms where the sessions were held.

Our hope with this project is to carry on the work that those first record producers and musicians began almost a century ago. Music connects people on more than an intellectual level: as we listen, we learn about other people and their worlds. We share their emotions, their thoughts and dreams, the rhythms of their bodies and their environments. In the 1920s, listeners all over America heard new sounds on recordings and were inspired to send their own music out in response. Our goal is to extend that web of connections across space and time.

The first chapter of this book traces the journeys and experiments of the "record men" in the 1920s, setting the scene by exploring where the music came from and how it came to us. Then we set off across America, tracing ten of our most treasured artists back to their homes, meeting their families, looking through their photo albums, and listening to their stories. Finally, we bring the story full circle by inviting the musical descendants of those artists to relive the experience of recording under the conditions of the 1920s.

Our American epic started with the records—messages from a distant past that spoke to us of strange lives and magical places. Today those records sound better than ever, and mean more to us, but they no longer feel so distant or ancient. Going in search of old friends, we found new ones, and when we listen today, we are reminded both of a treasured past and of people and cultures that are very much alive in the present and looking toward the future. Much as it would have surprised the record men and musicians of the 1920s, the music they preserved has proved to be truly timeless.

I | THE FIRST TIME AMERICA HEARD HERSELF

Art Satherley, circa 1935

BERNARD: The late 1920s was a golden age of American record making. In part, that was due to radical new technology: the advent of electrical recording made it possible to record a much wider range of sounds and to put together portable studios and record in varied locations. But it was also a matter of necessity: radio was supplanting phonograph records as the main way pop music got into people's homes, so the record companies were forced to seek out alternative markets.

ART SATHERLEY (record producer for Paramount, QRS, ARC, and Columbia): Those were tough days, mister. Especially when radio started to come in. And you can put this on record for all times: the thing that saved the record industry of the great America was what is now commonly known as the rhythm and blues and the country and western. That's what saved the industry, and that is *it*.

Blind Lemon Jefferson, king of the Texas blues

BERNARD: To a great extent, it was a purely economic, entrepreneurial impulse. A good example is the Wisconsin Chair Company: they were making furniture, and that included phonograph cabinets, and they wanted to expand the market for phonographs—so they formed Paramount Records in 1917, with Art Satherley at the helm. In 1921 they began issuing discs of African American music, because they were a relatively small, new label, so they were looking for a new audience in that community. And since they knew very little about that community, they took out advertisements in African American newspapers, looking for people who wanted to sell records, and sometimes those agents would also recommend musicians—for example, in 1926 a store clerk in Dallas wrote to Paramount suggesting that they should record a local street singer named Blind Lemon Jefferson, so they did, and his records sold so well that dozens of other black singer-guitarists were soon being recorded all across the South.

ART SATHERLEY: Anybody could become an agent. All they did was to take ten records and send us four dollars and fifty cents, plus the postage: forty-five cents apiece, [and they sold them for] seventy-five cents, or what they could get—from what I understand, some of them could get three, four bucks apiece. It was so new for the people of America, both black and white, to be able to buy what they understood and what they wanted. . . . [The record company owners] had no idea of what a Negro in those days was singing and what he was talking about, and what country folk or people from Mississippi, Louisiana were singing. They thought it was a bunch of—let's not mention it.

RALPH PEER (record producer for Columbia, OKeh, and Victor): I believe that except for the First World War both the Negro and the hillbilly [music] would have been buried. . . . You had the thing of many Negroes going north to work in factories, many white people going north to work in any factory, 'cause they could make more money. That caused an intermixing, and then after the war ended, it was found that labor was much cheaper in the South, so this movement took place of opening cotton mills in Charlotte and Atlanta and what have you. So the standard of living of all these people was raised, and then they could buy phonographs, they could buy records.

The porters on Pullman trains would make a fortune just by carrying the records—they would pay a dollar apiece for 'em and sell 'em for two dollars, because the Negroes in the South had the money . . . their standard of living was being raised, so that led to the Negro record business and eventually it led to the hillbilly record business. This is an economic fact.

BERNARD: The record companies' attitude epitomized the sort of adventurous and rapacious American ideal of exploring and exploiting new territories. The music and musicians were a means to an end: what was on the records didn't matter, as long as they were selling. One of the things that struck me as I listened to interviews with the pioneering record men—Art Satherley, Ralph Peer, even Frank Walker, who had played with a little country band when he was young—is the lack of any strong emotion about the music: they talk about it very much as if they were harvesting a crop, and they don't have any particular emotion about the individual ears of corn. The only time I hear any of these major record men talking with some degree of fondness about an artist is when the artist sold exceptionally well.

At its worst, this makes the process feel like a sort of brutal capitalist mining operation, with these individuals singing their heartfelt songs and the companies treating them like a vein of coal or iron ore. But at the same time, that relationship is what produced this fantastic artistic period: the record men were not emotional about the music, but they were very practical about getting the recordings made to a high standard and distributed quickly, and reaching the largest possible audience. Meanwhile, the emotional side of it, the content and the feeling, was left almost entirely with the artists. That's something you see in various periods of American popular music—it happened again with rock 'n' roll, and with hip-hop—these moments when the record companies are trying to exploit something they don't understand, so there is this period of experimentation and freedom, where they're taking chances on unusual artists and not exerting much control over how those artists sound. After a while those lines get blurred, and the record companies start to have artistic ideas about the material, and try to make it more uniform and standardized. But those first exploratory periods are very exciting.

Ralph and Anita Peer on the road

Example of a typical acoustic recording session, 1914

The late 1920s were particularly exciting, because for the first time the record companies were ranging out into what they regarded as the hinterlands and recording all sorts of styles that had never before been thought of as professional or popular music. Ralph Peer was really the pioneer in that effort—he had produced the first huge hit for the African American market in 1920, with Mamie Smith's "Crazy Blues," and in 1924 he produced the first major country hit when he recorded Fiddlin' John Carson in Atlanta. He also established the practice of marketing those records in separately numbered series, so that dealers would know which records were intended for African American or rural buyers—what are often called the "Race" and "hillbilly" lines, though I prefer not to use those terms because I find them insulting.

Peer started making annual trips to Atlanta in 1923, and the next year added New Orleans, and he also did some sessions in St. Louis. But he was never happy with the quality of recordings he could get on the road using the old acoustic process—before 1926, records were made by using large, cone-shaped horns to transmit sound vibrations directly to the stylus that cut the master disc, and even in the most perfectly designed studios it was a very demanding and rather limited technology. When electrical recording came in, they could get vastly better quality recordings, and it made the process much more portable—though "portable" is a relative term: they would carry a whole truckload of equipment, including the electric amplifiers, which were quite big; the microphone, with a backup as well; a weight-driven lathe to cut the master discs; a supply of the thick wax discs they used for the original masters; and they also needed to carry their own wet cell batteries, because they couldn't rely on the local current being regular and any fluctuations would affect the recordings.

It was a cumbersome process, but the combination of new markets and technology, and the competition as more companies began issuing regional styles, prompted a dramatic increase in mobile recording. In 1927, Peer (who had recently switched from OKeh to Victor) added Memphis, Charlotte, Savannah, and Bristol, Tennessee, to his rounds—in the process making the first recordings of the Carter Family, Jimmie Rodgers, and the Memphis Jug Band—and over the next three years, until the Depression forced everyone to cut back, OKeh, Victor, Columbia, Vocalion, and Gennett all sent recording teams south.

FRANK WALKER (producer for Columbia): We recorded in dozens and dozens of different places, all the way from San Antonio to Houston and Dallas, and Johnson City, Tennessee; and Memphis, and Little Rock, and New Orleans, and Atlanta; everywhere. You would write down to various people that you'd heard about, and let it be known—it would be mentioned in the paper and the word would get around in churches and schoolhouses that somebody was going

Lydia Mendoza recording session
at the Texas Hotel, San Antonio, 1934

Frank Walker

to come down there for a recording. You'd talk to everybody around: who did they know that could fiddle, could play guitar, could sing. . . .

And these people would show up from sometimes eight and nine hundred miles away—how they got there I'll never know, and how they got back I'll never know. They never asked you for money. They didn't question anything at all. They just were happy to sing and play, and we were happy to have them—and mostly we saw that they had something to go back with.

They hadn't the slightest idea what it was all about, so you had to give them an atmosphere as if it was home. You didn't pick out any fancy spot to record in, you usually took the upstairs of some old building where it looked pretty terrible, and you didn't try to fix it up in any way at all. You hung some drapes or curtains around, and you brought in a little of the "mountain dew" to take care of the colds and any hoarseness that might happen, and also to remove a little of their fears. . . . You tried to make them feel at home, and we felt the only way we could ever get that was in their own native habitat. You couldn't have done it in New York.

In Atlanta, we recorded in a little hotel and we used to put the singers up and pay a dollar a day for their food and a place to sleep in another little old hotel. Then we would spend all the night going from one room to another, and they kept the place hopping all night in all the different rooms that they were in. It was a regular party. We'd sit up all night long and listen to them, and you'd talk with them, you said "We'll use this" and "We won't use that," and you timed it, and you rehearsed them the next morning, and you recorded them in the afternoon and the evening. It was a twenty-four-hour deal, seven days a week.

Their repertoire would consist of maybe eight or ten or twelve things that they did well, and that was all they knew. When you had picked out the three or four best things in their so-called repertoire, you were through with that man as an artist. It was a culling job, taking the best of what they had. You might come out with only two selections, or you might come out with six or eight, but you got everything that you thought they were capable of doing well and would be salable, and that was it—you forgot about them, said good-bye, and they went back home. They had made a phonograph record, and that was the next thing to being president of the United States in their mind.

Can You Sing or Play Old-Time Music?

Musicians of Unusual Ability --- Small Dance Combinations--- Singers --- Novelty Players, Etc.

Are Invited

To call on Mr. Walker or Mr. Brown of the Columbia Phonograph Company at 334 East Main Street, Johnson City, on Saturday, October 13th, 1928—9 A. M. to 5. P. M.

This is an actual try-out for the purpose of making Columbia Records.

You may write in advance to F. B. Walker, Care of John Sevier Hotel, Johnson City, or call without appointment at address and on date mentioned above.

ART SATHERLEY: I didn't just say "Sing this," and then go and have a drink somewhere. I spent my time in that studio, getting that record to the people of the world. . . . When I talked with those Negroes, I would figure them out. I would tell them something about my background as an immigrant [from England]. I would tell them what we had to expect. . . . Before they would sing a spiritual, I would ask, "Who has lost a loved one in the last year or so, step forward." Then I would say to the fellow that had some preaching experience, "Say a short prayer before we start recording." This was not an act, I might add. It was this ability to be an honest man, to give them what they wanted back. You just don't go in like animals and talk to people, whether they're white, black, pink, or any color. You need to know their life a little bit, and they need to know that you're not going to hurt them, too.

I would say I recorded a hundred thousand pieces since 1919 . . . but many of them were tryouts—I've recorded many a person all he had, then picked out what I thought would sell and thrown the rest out without even messing with it. If we found out we didn't think they'd make it, we'd cancel it and just save the copper.

You had to make three masters of everything, on wax. And either ship it to New York, or even if we were in New York we'd still make three masters. And we would pick the best out of

Columbia Records engineer with a Western Electric recording rack, circa 1926

Weight-driven recording lathe with Western recording rack

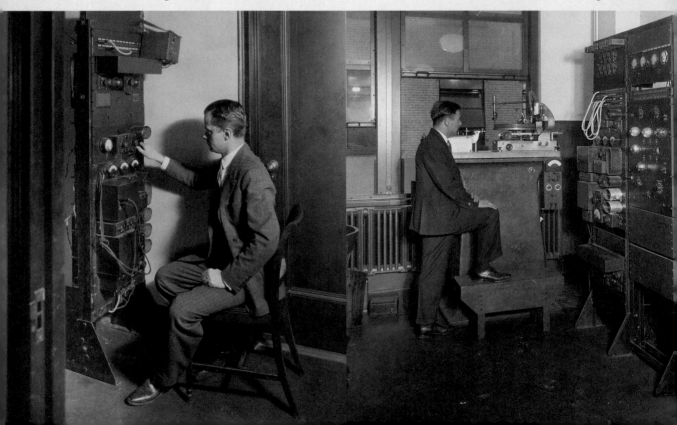

Diagram showing the Western Electric amplifier parts

the three, make the masters out of that one, and save the other two waxes until we were safe, in case we had an accident in the baths. . . .

BERNARD: The process of record making was quite complicated and labor intensive. During a recording session, the sound would be picked up by a microphone and filtered through the amplifier to a vibrating metal stylus, which was lowered onto a revolving wax disc. The stylus cut a spiral groove from the outer edge of the disc toward the center, engraving a pattern of vibrations in the sides of the groove. The wax master was then electroplated by covering it with a layer of graphite and lowering it into a plating bath, which was electrically charged. A layer of copper or nickel would be attracted to the graphite and gradually form on the master, exactly filling the grooves, and then you would peel off this plate, which was called the "father," and it was a negative of the original wax master, with the grooves sticking up. The father was then used to stamp a metal disc that was positive, like a finished record, which was called the "mother," and then the mother was used to stamp another generation of metal negatives, called "stampers," which you put on the press to stamp the finished records. The idea was to protect the original mother and father—the so-called metal parts—from being worn down in the course of producing thousands or millions of records.

In the course of the *American Epic* project, we were trying to hunt down original metal parts for the records we would be reissuing, and we discovered a rather strange thing: the vast majority of metal parts were lost or destroyed over the years, but the ones that survive, in a great many cases, are the unreleased takes rather than the issued ones. We haven't figured out why that would be, but in many instances when we listened to those alternate takes, they were better than the released version—not necessarily the performance, but the sound quality: generally the sound on the alternates was significantly louder and more present. The reason seems to be that they carefully analyzed each take before release, but they were making their decisions based not on the quality of the music or the sound, but on how well they would wear. The records that sound louder and more present would make the needle bounce around more in the groove, and if you were playing your records on an old Victrola with a steel needle, they would wear worse than a quieter performance—they'd sound great for the first few plays, but then would get dull and scratchy. So it seems that one of the main criteria for choosing one take over another wasn't artistic or emotional—it was just to create a durable commercial product, like a good work shoe.

That sounds cold-blooded, but this utterly commercial approach had some surprisingly positive effects on the music. One of the most important was that, rather than just recording whatever tunes people were playing at dances or on street corners, the record companies wanted novel, unique material. Ralph Peer, in particular, had a deal with Victor where the company didn't even pay him a salary but just let him publish all the songs he recorded—so his whole livelihood depended on finding artists who had original songs, or at least sufficiently original versions of older songs, so he could copyright and publish them. And that was an important innovation, because the commercial music business had previously been based on songwriters composing material but other people performing it. The new approach put a premium on artists who were not only expert musicians but could create or rework their own songs.

RALPH PEER: Finding the new stuff continuously, month after month, is not easy. We continued to insist on new material; we wouldn't let them record "Home, Sweet Home." We found out the hard way that we couldn't sell any of them—there's always been better records of "Home, Sweet Home."

These people would come in who could play a guitar very well and sing very well, and I'd test them out: "What other music have you got?"

"Well, I sing . . ." some song that was popular on record, some pop song.

"Do you have any music of your own?"

That was the test. If they said, "Well, no, but I can get some," I never bothered with them, they never got a chance. Maybe I threw out some of the best recording artists, but I certainly threw them out. . . .

Dock Walsh of the Carolina Tar Heels at a Victor recording session

June 6 1930.

Mr. L. L. Watson,
RCA Victor Co., Inc.,
153 E. 24th St.,
New York, N. Y.

Dear Loren:

Following is information regarding recordings made during the week ending
May 31st:

MEMPHIS JUG BAND, FOUR SELECTIONS:

I have already written you about"Bumble Bee Blues"which is a big hit on
Vocalian. Another Jug Band selection with vocal by Memphis Minnie is
"Meningitis Blues." As you probably know, there is a Meningitis epidemic
in this part of the Country.

WASHINGTON WHITE, NINE SELECTIONS:

This is a new Artist brought to Memphis by Ralph Lembo of Itta Bena, Miss.
The selection, "The Panama Limited", is a train piece played on the guitar
and it is intended that it should be coupled with BVE-59995, "The New Fris-
co Train". The four Blues selections are very good corn field type and
should have a big sale in the delta country. Selections BVE-62505 to
62508 are sacred selections done in Holy Roller style. We have nothing
else like this and I recommend a quick release of one of these records.

NAPOLEON & WASHINGTON, FIVE SELECTIONS:

BVE-59995 is intended for coupling with BVE-59996. The four Blues selections are sung by Napoleon Hairiston with accompaniment and other assistance
from Washington White. Napoleon was furnished by Mr. Ralph Lembo.

REV. M. H. HOLT & CONGREGATION, FOUR SELECTIONS:

BVE-62509 and BVE-62510 constitute a complete funeral service and burial
for Sister Jessie McClellan. Selection BVE-62511, "The Live Cat on the Line",
impressed me very favorably. Please pay particular attention to BVE-62512,
"The Beaver", as this may not be suitable for listing. The Rev. Holt was furnished by Mr. Ralph Lembo.

MEMPHIS MINNIE & KANSAS JOE, FOUR SELECTIONS:

These Artists have made a big hit on Vocalian records. BVE-59992 and BVE-
62539 are individualnumbers with both Minnie and Joe singing. BVE-62538 should
be coupled with BVE-62537 by Bessie & Minnie McCoy.

WHEELER & LAMB, EIGHT SELECTIONS:

I recommend that these selections be coupled in the same order in which they appear in the recording book.

OWEN BROTHERS & ELLIS, SIX SELECTIONS:

This is a male sacred quartet with a guitar accompaniment who have been very big sellers on Columbia. For the first release, I recommend BVE-62522, "Look on the Bright Beautiful Side".

PETE HERRING, TWO SELECTIONS:

This Artist was brought to us by Dr. Bailey of Winona, Miss., and these two selections are intended as a trial.

MISSISSIPPI 'POSSUM HUNTERS, FOUR SELECTIONS:

This is a three piece string band brought in by Dr. Bailey from Central Mississippi, no vocal. For the first release, I recommend BVE-62523 coupled with BVE-62524.

RAY BROTHERS, FOUR SELECTIONS:

A violin and guitar duet without vocal, brought in by Dr. Bailey. I recommend a quick release of BVE-62535, "Jake Leg Wobble", coupled with BVE-62531, Honeysuckle Waltz".

BESSIE & MINNIE MC COY, ONE SELECTION:

This is Memphis Minnie singing with her sister, Bessie. The coupling for this is BVE-62538.

MC INTORSH & AWING, FOUR SELECTIONS:

McIntorsh has previously recorded for both O. K. and Victor. I have put a woman's voice with him and think that we have something unusual in the way of sanctified records.

JOHN ESTES, TWO SELECTIONS:

JOHN ESTES & JAMES RACHEL, TWO SELECTIONS:

The vocal in these selections is by Rachel with assistance from Estes.

KAISER CLIFTON, FOUR SELECTIONS:

This is a new Artist having a good, high tenor blues voice.

GRINNEL GIGGERS, TWO SELECTIONS:

This is a string band without vocal from Manila, Ark. For Mr. Oberstein's information, a grinnel is a local species of fish and a gigger is one who gigs or spears said fish.

LEROY ROBERSON, TWO SELECTIONS:

This is a new Artist imitating Jimmie Rodgers. He has very little voice but an

Ralph Peer Memphis recording session notes

Weight-driven Scully cutting lathe, circa 1920s

By insisting on new material and leaning towards artists that could produce it for us, their own compositions, that created the so-called hillbilly business, and also the [Race] business. I do take full credit, and this is the basis for the whole business. I never recorded an established selection; I always insisted on getting artists who could write their own music. Now that comes right up to the business of today—the record business of today is founded on that.

BERNARD: It really was a sea change not only in recording practices but in the whole concept of popular music—even perhaps in the whole concept of what music was or could be. It is very hard to imagine ourselves back before that time, to think about what it was like when virtually all the commercial music, all the music one would hear at concerts or on records, or in most performance venues, was created by a small group of composers in a few major cities, and performed by people who tended to have at least some formal training. It was a very generic world: in a lot of ways all the professional entertainers were performing this quite narrow range of material in a quite narrow range of styles, and they tended to sound quite similar to one another. And meanwhile, there were all these other people making unique, distinctive music in their communities, but it was not being recorded or disseminated. Like the Carter Family: they were living up in the hills, making this wild, wonderful music, but when they bought records, they heard pretty much the same selections they would have heard in New York or Texas, or even in London.

MAYBELLE CARTER: My husband had a Victrola and a gang of records when we got married . . . popular records like "Who?" and all those songs back then, which were very popular—"Dinah," and I can recall a few [others] that he had. We didn't have too many songs like we sang, just Vernon Dalhart and Riley Puckett. There might of been another one or two, but I don't recall any. . . . In fact, I just didn't think too much about it. A record was a record to me, if I picked it up and played it. Of course, some of them I probably liked better than the others, but then you didn't have too many to choose from, you know.

Making Records *the* New Victor Way

Orthophonic Recording! From one to a thousand voices or instruments *faithfully* recorded ~ just as they sing!

BERNARD: When the record companies began releasing these new styles of music— many of which were really quite old styles of music but had never been part of the commercial music world—it was this marvelously circular process, because people could hear other people like themselves, and that would inspire them to want to make their own recordings, or just to think differently about themselves and their communities. One of the amazing things about this story is how quickly the records reached even very remote areas, because people were hungry to hear something they could relate to in that way. Of course, that was the idea—to create these new markets, to prompt new sorts of people to buy records and to buy phonographs. Frank Walker actually talked about setting up listening sessions, to let country people know about what was available and also as sort of rough demographic experiments, to see what sorts of records they liked.

So all those things came together, for all those reasons, and even though the reasons might have been commercial and the rewards were rarely distributed as fairly as one might like, and the impulses were not always virtuous, the result was a new concept of popular music in its purest, most democratic form. As Art Satherley paraphrased Abraham Lincoln: music of the people, by the people, and for the people.

FRANK WALKER: [Here is] a little bit of a story as to how you sold hillbilly records to hill guys: back in the middle '20s, I had a couple of new artists and I happened to be traveling down through there, and I landed in a little town called Corbin, Kentucky. It was a sort of a railroad town as I recall it, and I went into a little store that was a sort of a general store, and he did sell some phonograph records, and he had a machine in there. So I went in and I said, "Let's try out something. . . . Let's put up some seats here in the back, it won't take much. We'll take some planks and so forth and we'll make little ring seats like they have at a ball game. And we'll put the phonograph out in the front, and then we'll make some signs that we'll put on the window, and we'll invite the folks to come in Saturday afternoon and listen to the new phonograph records."

He said, "I like the idea."

We had room for about sixty people—I think we had a hundred and sixty that showed up. We filled the seats and they all stood around, and we had the appropriate little box with the sawdust in it so that we didn't get too much tobacco juice on the floor. And I started and played two or three records that I'm sure that they knew about already. Then I put on this new record and played it all the way through—one that nobody had ever heard before, a new release that I had that was coming out, but I just wanted to try it out. So I played it, and then I said, "How many of you people would like to own this record, have it for yourself?"

Everybody held their hands up.

"Now," I said, "how many of you would like to buy this record for seventy-five cents?" And I would say out of maybe the hundred twenty-five or thirty people there that maybe twenty or twenty-five held their hand up.

I said, "What's the matter with the rest of you, don't you like it?"

They said, "Yes, [but] we've got no money." Which was the story. They all liked it, you see, and all wanted it, but they didn't have the money. So the result is that you'd then be nice about it and give them one, because you found out exactly what you wanted to know, and you were going to sell up to the extent of the amount of money that people had to spend.

[Later on,] the falloff in the sale of hillbilly music was due to one thing and that was the Depression—because remember: who was affected most by the Depression in the '30s was your country people. They didn't have the money to buy. But it came back—you give them the money, and they'll buy 'em. . . .

I started going around the country and gathering people off the street by giving them a slip of paper and telling them that we wanted their opinion on a certain phonograph record, if they'd be at such a place at a certain time in the afternoon. We would bring in people all up the ladder—from the bank president to the street cleaner—and they would listen to a record, and you'd watch the expression on their face. And we were able to judge then, because you were playing to America.

One of the four Western Electric field recording trunks with condenser microphone, cutting heads, tubes, intercom, and control box

2

I'LL GET A BREAK SOMEDAY:
WILL SHADE AND THE MEMPHIS JUG BAND

Memphis, with the Mississippi and Riverside Drive by moonlight

BERNARD: Memphis has always seemed to me like the musical heart of America. W. C. Handy was there in the teens and made blues into a sort of national craze, and then you have the Memphis Jug Band and all the musicians who recorded there in the 1920s and '30s, then the postwar scene with Sun Records and Elvis Presley, then the soul explosion with Stax and Hi Records in the 1960s and '70s, as well as more esoteric things like Big Star.

Memphis has a special allure for British people, and we have a particular connection to the jug bands, because if you were growing up in my mum's era, the 1950s, the big popular music was skiffle. Everyone was in a skiffle group, with the streamline bass [aka washtub or tea chest bass], washboard, guitars, kazoos. That music permeated Britain—even the Beatles started out as a skiffle band—so those sounds are very, very familiar. In fact, I originally thought "skiffle" was a British term for our own hybrid of American blues, jazz, and hillbilly music, but it turned out that the word was coined in the 1920s for jug band music, and those bands were already playing a hybrid of all those styles.

I first heard the Memphis Jug Band when I was thirteen. I used to go to the British Phonographic Institute, where they tried to archive every record ever made, and I heard a compilation of some Memphis Jug Band tracks, and I thought they sounded terrific. Their records are the most eclectic, colorful, and exciting African American music from the early twentieth century. It's like a mixture of everything from raw, gritty blues to ballads and pop songs, and the beats are fantastic, and it just seems to completely transcend time.

I was doubly interested in Will Shade because, along with leading that band, he was kind of the kingpin of this music scene. When Ralph Peer went to Memphis for the first time in February 1927, the Memphis Jug Band was the main group he recorded, and their records sold really well and kick-started a whole era of recording there. But Peer also used Shade as a talent

The Memphis Jug Band with Will Shade
(jug) and Charlie Burse (tenor guitar)

scout to find other local artists. So, through the Memphis Jug Band and Will Shade, that led to all these other people getting recorded: Jim Jackson, Furry Lewis, Frank Stokes, Gus Cannon. . . . To me, he's sort of the key to that whole scene.

So I started exploring around Memphis, trying to find any relatives of Will Shade or anyone who knew him—literally going around town asking the oldest people I could find if there was anybody who remembered him. And I didn't have any luck at all. I had the sense that Memphis—at least that aspect of Memphis—is sort of a vanished world. But then I was talking with my friend Garth Cartwright in London, and he said, "You should speak to Charlie Musselwhite. He was a friend of Will Shade and used to go to his apartment and learn music from him." So he gave me Charlie's number, and I could tell immediately that Charlie was delighted to get a call about Will Shade.

Furry Lewis (bottom row, far left) *and friends in Memphis*

Charlie Musselwhite, age eighteen

CHARLIE MUSSELWHITE: I met Will when I was about eighteen. A friend of mine, George Mitchell, he lived in Atlanta and he came to Memphis and sought out Will Shade, and he took me over there, and I was just hanging out there every chance I could.

Where Will lived was like in the middle of a block—you'd go in an alley, and then there'd be little pathways and a whole neighborhood *inside* the block. It was a two-story apartment building, it had one bathroom at the end of the hall for each floor, and he had the last two rooms upstairs. He had a potbelly stove, and his wife, Jennie Mae, would lay up in the bed all day with her little glass of Golden Harvest sherry wine and smoking cigarettes that she would roll. And Will would sit by the window in a chair so he could see everybody coming up and down the alley and have conversations with them, and maybe they would come up and bring a bottle with them, and if there was a musician, maybe they'd come up and play something.

You never knew who was going to show up. There was musicians coming all the time: there was a guy named Harmonica Joe—I later found out his real name was Coy Love and he'd recorded for Sun Records—and Son Smith, who was a blind trumpet player; and Red Robey, the fiddle player; and Little Bit, whose real name was Laura Dukes. Willie B., whose real name was Willie Borum, he showed me how to play harmonica on a rack with the guitar. Earl Bell, Abe McNeil . . . Just people coming by to pay their respects to Will Shade, 'cause even though he was down on his luck, he was still a famous man to them.

Will liked to be comfortable, so he'd wear slippers around the house and just a pair of slacks. He often wouldn't wear a shirt, or he'd wear just an undershirt. He'd had a stroke, so his right arm would shake a little bit; he had trouble picking the guitar with his right hand, but he could strum and he could chord with his left hand fine. So he showed me lots of chords and I listened to him playing harmonica and tried to duplicate what he was doing. He just loved it that I was interested in learning his music, so he was always encouraging me and pushing me to get it right and play it better. We'd just play. It wasn't like he would say, "Now it's time for you to learn this." We'd just sit around and he'd play whatever he felt like playing, and I'd play along with him, either harmonica or guitar. We'd just have fun.

The stairs to Will Shade's apartment   *Will Shade's potbelly stove*

It wasn't always about music. Sometimes we'd just sit around listening to the ball game on the radio, or we'd talk about politics, or life, or tell jokes and laugh, or somebody might come by with a problem to discuss—people like Will and Furry Lewis, they were like the sages of the neighborhood.

On one hand it was really poor—I mean, like, squalor. But on the other hand it was this energetic, totally alive, wonderful place to be, with some really good friends, and we all had a great time. He cooked on that potbelly stove, and I swear to God the best hamburger I ever had in my life, Will Shade cooked it. We'd sit around and have really just jam sessions and passing the bottle, or on real hot days you'd have a pot filled with ice and water—like a dipping cup, but a big pot—and we'd pass that around, drinking ice water in between drinking Golden Harvest sherry wine. That was the popular drink: it was very affordable, and it did the trick.

I don't remember Will talking about his family. I just remember him talking about being raised by his grandmother—he was called "Son Brimmer" because his grandmother's name was Brimmer and she called him "Son"—and I remember him saying that his mom taught him harmonica. He told me he first learned guitar from a guy named Tee Wee Blackman. He was, as he put it, running up and down Beale Street, and he ran into this guy named Tee Wee Blackman playing guitar, and he wanted to play guitar, so he got one and started learning

Will Shade and his wife, Jennie Mae Clayton

Will Shade and friends at his apartment with a bottle of Golden Harvest sherry wine

from him. He was a young man and Tee Wee was an old man, and the first tune he learned from Tee Wee Blackman was "Newport News Blues." And that was the first tune he taught me, when I was a young guy and Will Shade was an older man.

I'M GOING TO NEWPORT NEWS, MAMA, GONNA CATCH A BATTLESHIP ACROSS THE DOGGONE SEA.

I'M GOING TO NEWPORT NEWS, MAMA, GONNA CATCH A BATTLESHIP ACROSS THE DOGGONE SEA.

FOR, LORD, THE WOMAN THAT I'M LOVING, GREAT GOD, PARTNER, DO NOT CARE FOR ME.

—MEMPHIS JUG BAND, "NEWPORT NEWS BLUES," 1927

Will Shade and Willie Borum

Beale Street, 1906

WILL SHADE: I was born in Memphis, Tennessee. Born in 1893.* Some people said that I wasn't that old, but I am. 'Course, I can't go by what people say. . . .

How I learnt to play music, I learnt it the hard way. I learnt from the stump on up. Grew up like a willow tree, and I learnt my music thataway. My daddy was a musician, a guitar picker, and a shoemaker, [but] the real first one I learned from was my mother. She learnt me how to play "On the Road Again"—"Natural-born eastman, on the road again." She learnt me that and I come from that to "Going 'round and 'round, me and my baby gonna move, Alabama bound."

I first started on a harmonica, next started on a guitar. Then from there on, I come on up a little further. Got around a joint you call Pee Wee's. Nothing but bootlegging whiskey, crap shooting going on, and so forth like that. Got around the underworld people, and after I got around the underworld people, why, I learnt how to play the blues.

I met Tee Wee Blackman and I got some ideas from Tee Wee Blackman. [Then] I began to

---

* Most sources give Shade's birth year as 1898.

pull out for myself. I rigged me a little old three-piece band. After rigging up a three-piece band, why I met a feller by the name of Roundhouse, but his name was Elijah—old man, about sixty-five years old. And so we got together. He was playing a bottle—wasn't playing a gallon jug, just had one of them old whiskey bottles you pick up anywhere; he was playing that. So finally we thought it over, we said, "Let's get a gallon jug." I bought me a jug, a crocker jug. . . . I just got me some water and raised my jug and made my own tone. As I raised the water, the water raised the tone; I lowered the water, lowered the tone.

CHARLIE MUSSELWHITE: A jug band is some guys making music off of cheap instruments. They couldn't afford, like, trumpets and fancy brass instruments, so they had, like, a washboard and they had a kazoo, a jug, and Will Shade took an old oil can and made a tub bass out of it with a broom handle and some kind of cord, and harmonicas and guitars—just affordable instruments that they could get their hands on.

WILL SHADE: I doubles: I play a harmonica, guitar, also I got a can—some people call it a garbage can, but it's a streamline bass. I put a little stick up on it . . . put this string on it and shellacked it with some shellac. It worked very well, but it gave my fingers the devil, 'cause it cut my fingers, that shellac did. So I got rid of the shellac, wouldn't use nothing but the plain old fish cord. Then I got a tone: *boom, boom, boom, boom*. I learnt the ideas of how to pull the stick backwards and forwards to get my tone. I learnt how to run a scale on that, [and] by running a scale, that gave me ideas. . . . I learnt some of Andy [Kirk]'s pieces, some of Duke Ellington's, some of Cab [Calloway]'s, and some of all them big stars. I learnt a gang of those pieces.

CHARLIE MUSSELWHITE: They wanted to be able to play anything for any audience: whoever they were playing for, and what-

Top: *Will Shade blowing a gallon jug*
Bottom: *Pee Wee's nightclub*

"I HEARD A GOOD STORY"

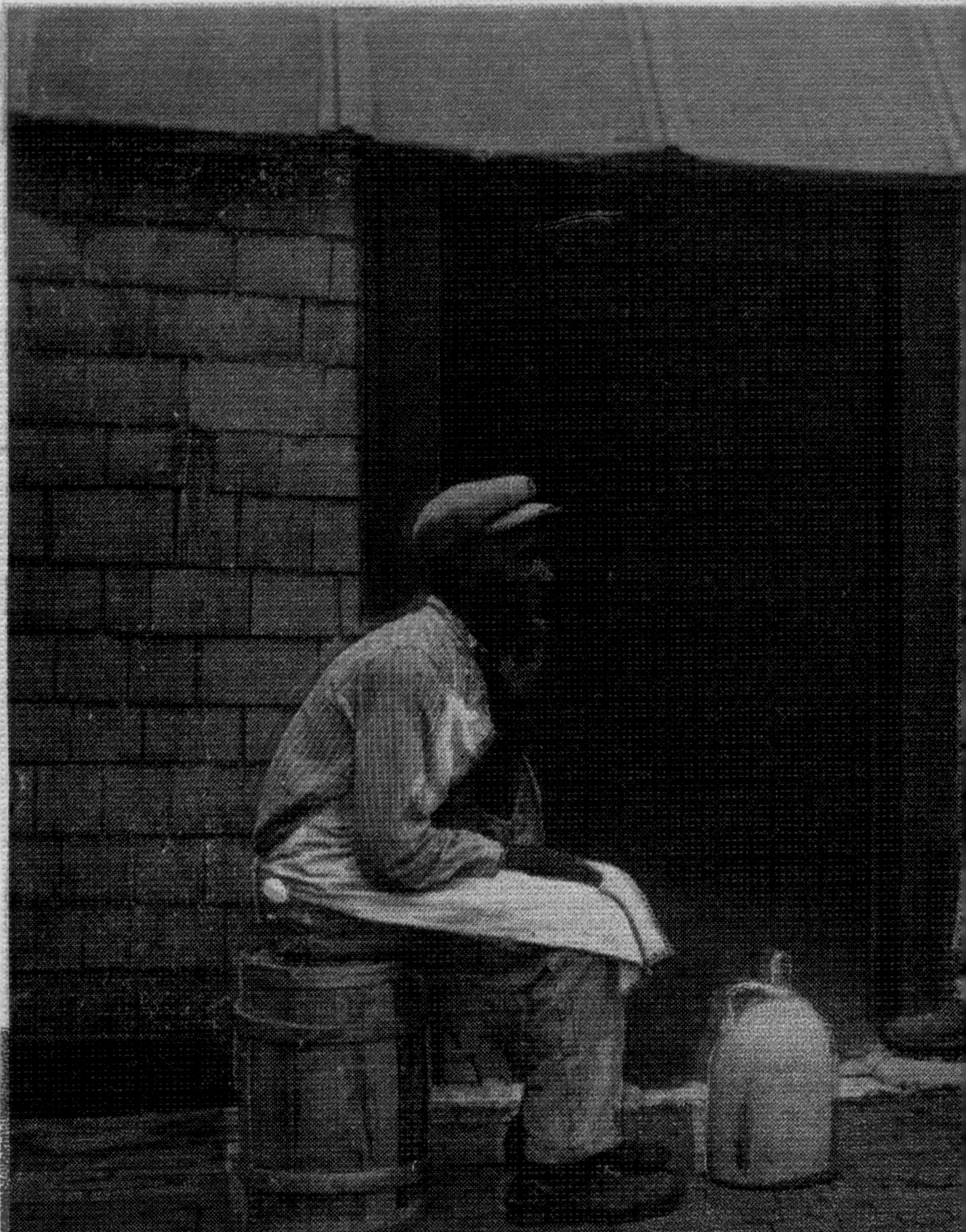

Will Shade with his streamline bass

ever they wanted to hear, they wanted to be able to provide that. They would play on the steamboats for white audiences, they'd play for black audiences, they'd play in the Peabody Hotel, they played for the mayor of Memphis. Will Shade told me that he once played for the president—I forget which one, it might have been one of the Roosevelts.

It was all his show; he was the man. He picked the music, or he wrote the music. If the musicians weren't cutting it, he fired them and other people got hired. He could have replaced anybody in the band, got other musicians, it would still be the Memphis Jug Band, with his sound, his music, his ideas.

The Jug Band got so well known that they had more gigs than they could do, so Will Shade created two Memphis Jug Bands—he'd have one playing in one part of town and one playing in another part of town, so they could get all that money. I don't know if Will would run over and play with one, then run over and play with the other one or not, but that's how in demand they were.

WILL SHADE: The story about how I got to make the first record: I was going down Beale Street playing the "Memphis Jug Band Blues." Charlie Williamson [a popular local cornet player] was at the Beale Street Palace. He picked me up on it and he turned me over to Mr. Peer, R. S. Peer. He was a junior superintendent for the Victor company, and after he picked me up at the Palace Theater, we made the records at the McCall Building on McCall Street. The first records I made was "Newport News," "Sun Brimmer's Blues," "Stingy Woman," and the "Memphis Jug Band Blues."

After I made the Memphis Jug Band famous, then everybody in Memphis had a jug band! They had the South Memphis Jug Band, North Memphis Jug Band, East Memphis Jug Band, West Memphis Jug Band. . . . They didn't know which kind of jug band was the right band, so we had little arguments. Finally they faded away, and I'm still here: the Memphis Jug Band, the old standby.

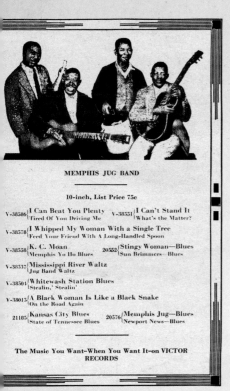

MEMPHIS JUG BAND

10-inch, List Price 75c

V-38586 {I Can Beat You Plenty / Tired Of You Driving Me

V-38551 {I Can't Stand It / What's the Matter?

V-38578 {I Whipped My Woman With a Single Tree / Feed Your Friend With A Long-Handled Spoon

V-38558 {K. C. Moan / Memphis Yo Ho Blues

20552 {Stingy Woman—Blues / Sun Brimmers—Blues

V-38537 {Mississippi River Waltz / Jug Band Waltz

V-38501 {Whitewash Station Blues / Stealin,' Stealin'

V-38013 {A Black Woman Is Like a Black Snake / On the Road Again

21185 {Kansas City Blues / State of Tennessee Blues

20576 {Memphis Jug—Blues / Newport News—Blues

The Music You Want–When You Want It–on VICTOR RECORDS

Memphis Jug Band advertisement, 1929

WHEN I GET BACK TO MEMPHIS, YOU CAN BET I'LL STAY,

WHEN I GET BACK TO MEMPHIS, YOU CAN BET I'LL STAY,

AND I AIN'T GONNA LEAVE UNTIL THAT JUDGMENT DAY.

—MEMPHIS JUG BAND, "GOING BACK TO MEMPHIS," 1930

The McCall Building

ALLISON: It was interesting being in Memphis. When you look at old photographs, you see a busy river full of steamboats and cargo boats, bustling, but when you're actually there, it's very quiet—I think in the whole time we were there, we saw one solitary cargo boat going down, so it's just like a vague memory of what might have been there in the past. I can imagine how vibrant it must have been back in its heyday, with bustling stores like [A.] Schwab on Beale Street, and the grand Peabody Hotel, where we stayed. So much incredible music has come from Memphis through the decades, from the original musicians coming up the Mississippi on the steamboats, then Sun Studio, Elvis Presley, and Stax, and many more. It's such a rich history, with so much to explore. It also made me sad because Jeff Buckley, son of our good friend Mary, drowned there in the Mississippi River, which has really strong currents, and as we filmed there you could feel the power of the mighty river, and its danger was palpable.

Will Shade (guitar) and Dewey Corley (bass) playing by the Mississippi

BERNARD: When we got to Memphis, Allison and I went out scouting the city at night, looking for the right location to film our interview with Charlie, and we had the addresses of all the clubs that had been popular in Memphis at the time the Jug Band was playing—Pee Wee's, the Monarch, the Panama, the Hole in the Wall, and all these different places—and all of them had been knocked down, bar one: the only one standing was the Monarch Club, right next to W. C. Handy Park.

ALLISON: We looked through the windows, and it seemed very little changed from its heyday, with redbrick walls and the remnants of the old wooden bar—but there were rows of bicycles and scooters lined up, all identical, and they were black police bicycles and police scooters. And it turned out that what used to be one of the most rowdy and vibrant clubs back in the '20s is now the police station.

We asked the police if we could film in there, and they hadn't realized it used to be a club, but they were really helpful and agreed. So we did our interview with Charlie there. It was quite

A record store and shoe shine on Beale Street

wonderful: Charlie was talking about how he felt the ghosts of the past were in there, and it really did feel like that, like it was the only place left where you could actually touch that past.

CHARLIE MUSSELWHITE: Beale Street today ain't the Beale Street I knew when I was a kid. Today there's still a lot of nightlife there, a lot of clubs and live music, and there's a lot of tourists go there. But when I was a kid it was a different kind of nightlife: there was all kinds of back rooms and clubs and cafés and pawnshops, and it was going night and day, around the clock. Great places to eat, lot of musicians; there was a whole neighborhood of people that lived round there that I knew, and now it's all pretty much gone.

When I was a kid, before they had malls and things, you'd always come downtown to go shopping or go to a movie or anything special like that. And before I'd go home, I'd walk around downtown or down on Beale Street, 'cause I knew eventually I'd find one of these street singers, one of these guys playing guitar on the corner for tips. I was fascinated by these guys, they just seemed so colorful to me, and I liked the words they were singing and the way the

Memphis Jug Band advertisements for "Coal Oil Blues" (April 1928) and "Cocaine Habit Blues" (September 1930)

music sounded. It was blues, and the way it sounded was how I felt. I liked all the other kinds of music, rockabilly and gospel and everything, but blues was the words from my heart, you know; it really meant something to me.

I remember Will Shade talking about Beale Street being wild and rough, and I remember even reading about it in the paper where Memphis was the murder capital of the world at one time. Everybody from the past, the old-timers I knew that talked about Beale Street, would talk about it being rough like that. Only Will Shade made it way more colorful than anybody I heard describe it.

WILL SHADE: Oh, they used to have a wonderful time 'round here in Memphis, Tennessee. . . . We was running all night long: chop suey'd be running, crap shoot be going on, loaded dice, and blank dice, shoot all kind of dice—four to eleven, six to eleven, and four deuces, four treys, and all such as that. The Monarch was running and crap games was going on. They had a good time, used to have pistols popping and cut throats, watch stealing and snatching. Pickpockets and everything . . . Sportin' class of woman running up and down the street all night long, and getting knocked in the head with bricks, and hatchets and hammers, pocketknives and razors and so forth like that, running down to the foot of Beale Street, make some of them run off in the river and drown. . . .

Roustabouts on the boats would come in at three and four and five o'clock in the morning when the boats come in, the *Kate Adams*—used to call that a woman's boat on the water. All the women would follow that boat, just pay fifty cent for cabin fare and ride that boat from Memphis to Rosedale, and that's the way they made their money, going up and down the river. They'd come back in; they wore nation sacks in them days. I don't know if you know what a nation sack is—they used to wear the money twixt their legs. They'd put on a sack, tie it around their waist, put the money in there. . . . They'd have so much money when they'd get back to Memphis, they'd be humpbacked, they couldn't straighten up.

Used to be a place on Beale Street they called the Monarch. And it was a crap-shooting joint. And another place called the Red Onion, and another place called the Venus. Prizefights there; used to prizefight so hard there they'd break one another's necks—knock one another down, knock them out of the ring, break their necks, all such as that.

There was so much excitement happening down on Beale Street, it'd take me a year and a day to tell you about all that excitement. It wasn't nothing too bad for you to see somebody's throat cut. That was the main part, you'd always see somebody get knocked in the head, and the ambulances—J. T. Hinton, and Thompson Brothers, and Qualls—all of them, they'd be in a line, they never would have had to call them. They'd line up because they knew what was gonna happen that Saturday night, and they all would be together, just lined up to race at the bodies. You wasn't dead, the ambulance had two drivers on there. One driver'd get back and take a needle and stick it in your arm, and you'd be dead when you get to the hospital. . . . They'd come and feel your pulse, and like that, say, "Oh, he's dead, take him over to the morgue. . . ." Oh, they had a million ways to make money.*

---

* The ambulances were owned by funeral companies—they often doubled as hearses—and presumably the payment for taking someone to the hospital was less than the funeral home could make if the client was ready for their services.

Always has had a good time around here. Until Prohibition all broke up and they put the bonded whiskey back, then that broke up that law. Run all the bootleggers out of town; the moonshiners, they had to bottle it up and go.

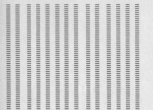

WHEN I HAD MONEY, HAD FRIENDS FOR MILES AROUND,

NOW I'M BROKE, SICK AND HUNGRY, NONE OF MY FRIENDS CAN BE FOUND.

BUT I'LL GET A BREAK, YES, SOMEWHERE BABY, BEFORE LONG.

—WILL SHADE, "I'LL GET A BREAK SOMEDAY," FROM A PRIVATE RECORDING BY CHARLIE MUSSELWHITE, 1963

CHARLIE MUSSELWHITE: Even after I moved to Chicago I kept coming back to Memphis regularly, and I'd go to see Will Shade. I'd always make that a point to go and see him, and I tried to give him some money or I'd always bring him a drink—he always wanted that Golden Harvest sherry wine. He loved to hear about what I was doing. He'd always ask me to play, see how I was advancing, if I was getting any better. I think he was real proud that I was his student and had continued to keep getting better and actually had started getting little gigs and things in Chicago.

The last time I went to see him, he was no longer living in that building, and there was a lady named "Yaller"—you know, for yellow. Somebody told me, "Yaller's across the street and Will Shade's living with her, on Hernando." I went over there to that apartment and Yaller took me into a little room in the back he had. He was real weak, and he had fell up against a heater, and he was so weak he couldn't move away from the heater, and it burned his arm really bad. He had all this stuff he was putting on it, and he was sitting on the bed, and we had a nice talk. He asked me to play him some harmonica, and I played, and he said, "Oh, boy, you sounded better than last time I heard. You've been learning all them Chicago licks." Which I had.

Charlie Musselwhite

When it came time I had to go, he was so weak he couldn't get his feet up on the bed, so I put his feet up for him and left, hoping I'd get back to see him again. But that was the last time I saw him.

Charles Brown used to say, "Dead noses can't smell roses—bring me flowers while I'm alive." But Will Shade didn't get that. I just wish I could somehow get in some kind of machine, go back and get Will Shade, and show him how all his records have been released and how people all around the world are interested in jug band music. Because he had a huge, tremendous effect on American music.

Will Shade

He knew that he was good and he had respect for what he did—and he didn't say so, 'cause he didn't, like, whine or complain, but I think he secretly felt like he should have gotten a better deal, you know. And I do, too.

BERNARD: Since Will was Charlie's mentor, we thought it would be a great idea to visit Will's grave and film Charlie playing a little tune for Will and leaving a harmonica at the gravesite. So we drove out to the cemetery where he was buried, a little ways outside of Memphis, but when we arrived with Charlie and the film crew, there were four or five police cars parked at the gates and policemen standing around. They wouldn't tell me what was going on, but I called the police chief and he said that the owners of the cemetery had been moving bodies around, removing tombstones, burying people on top of other people, and doing loads of nefarious activities. So the whole cemetery had been turned into a crime scene, and he said they would not be admitting visitors for at least a year.

CHARLIE MUSSELWHITE: Only in Memphis. And, growing up here, I'm not real surprised. . . . But, you know, something tells me that Will Shade arranged all this. With his association with old-style Memphis hoodoo, he's saying, "You didn't come and see me when you had a chance, all those years I was alive, so I ain't letting you in today."

VE

Orthophonic Recording

"HIS MASTER'S VOICE"

VICTOR

Orthophonic
Recording

20877–B

THE WANDERING BOY

(A. P. Carter)

The Carter Family

Singing with auto-harp and guitar

VICTOR TALKING MACHINE CO.
Camden, N.J.

VE

3 IN THE SHADOW OF CLINCH MOUNTAIN:
THE CARTER FAMILY

A. P. and Sara Carter on their farm

* *

BERNARD: When we began our journey we were hoping to find some clues to the lesser-known artists we admired, but more than that we wanted to get a sense of how the music emerged from particular places and communities. The Carter Family's story is central to the whole notion of country music, and it has been told in many ways, but we were particularly interested in them because so much of early country music was recorded by male artists, and to us the Carter Family is very much a female group. People speak of the importance of A. P. Carter as a song collector, but when you listen to the interviews with Sara and Maybelle, you realize that many of the songs were theirs, and they were doing most of the arranging and playing all the instruments—from the beginning the group was really built around Sara's voice and Maybelle's instrumental skills. But then again, when we were talking with the family, they all spoke of A.P. as the driving force, and he also is such an interesting, peculiar character.

ALLISON: Our first step was to call John Carter Cash, who had come to our filming sessions in Los Angeles, and he said we should talk with Dale Jett and Fern Salyer—Dale is a grandson of A. P. and Sara Carter, and Fern is A.P.'s niece. We immediately got on the phone to Dale, and he met us in Bristol, and he and Fern were absolutely wonderful souls. We drove around with him, seeing where the Carters grew up, the church where A.P. used to sing. It was really beautiful country—leafy, green, absolutely gorgeous—but also very isolated. Just to get from one house to the next was often a mile or more, and there was very little work. Everyone we met clearly cared very deeply about this place, and loved it, but it was not an easy place to make a living.

DALE JETT: Poor Valley—as the name implies, it's pretty rugged terrain. Hillside farming is about all's you can do around here—"struggling like a hillside farmer," if you've ever heard that expression. . . . My father had to move away from here and work in the automobile industry. My wife's father moved away. I myself, I work construction, and I've worked as far away as California, New York, Florida—white lines and green signs are kinda the norm.

In A. P. Carter's day and Sara and Maybelle's, everybody had a few chickens, a hog, maybe a milk cow, maybe a goat. Most people had an old coonhound or a squirrel dog. They'd eat coons, possums, squirrels, rabbit. A.P. done a little bit of farming, he sold fruit trees, he done a little bit of sawmilling. He worked for the railroad, cutting crossties. He tried a lot of things to make a living.

A.P. was born just across what we call the Knob, or Pine Ridge. That homeplace was the only house in that valley; I guess maybe two rooms downstairs, one room upstairs, and they raised seven or eight children in that little cabin, which is pretty common around here. He went to school at a little place right down from Mt. Vernon Church—they called it Friendly Grove School—and he went maybe to the third grade. You know, seventh or eighth grade was about as far as about anybody went back then—you got about that age, it's time to work.

FERN SALYER: When he went to school, a lot of the kids would make fun of him, they'd laugh at him. . . . He was real shaky, his hands would shake, and that was due to Grandma, when she was carrying him, there was a storm and she was out under an apple tree and that lightning went right along the ground with her and it scared her to death, and that's why they thought he had the shaky hands. That happened before he was born.

My grandmother had a brother named Flanders Bays, and he taught singing lessons. He'd go to the churches and schools and different places and teach 'em. He taught shape notes, and A.P. started going to that. He went to Uncle Flanders's singing schools a lot.

He would walk all the way across that mountain—it's a really big mountain, but he had a path, and he'd walk across the mountain. Sometimes some of the younger people would go. They'd take their lunch, because it took a while to get across there. That's where he met Aunt Sara.

DALE JETT: Sara was raised by Mil Nickels—they called him "Uncle Mil"—and Aunt Susie. I don't know the complete story of that, but her parents apparently died when she was young, and she was raised by them.

Sara Carter, age thirteen

SARA CARTER: I was born in eighteen and ninety-eight, July the twenty-first, in Wise County, Virginia. They called it the Flatwoods, near Coeburn. My mother died when I was about two years old. She died and they brought me over to my uncle Nickels. My dad, he used to work at a sawmill . . . he just brought us over there.

A.P.'s related to the Nickels, and just straight across Clinch Mountain—it was about eight or nine mile, if you walked across the mountain. He came in there at his aunt Susie Nickels, where I was a-staying. He came over to see her. And when he walked in, I was standing, singing "Engine 143."

DALE JETT: A.P. was selling fruit trees in that area—Nickelsville, Big Moccasin, Copper Creek— and he went up the holler one evening and said he heard the prettiest singing that he'd ever heard, like an angelic voice. It just pulled him up the holler, and it was Sara. She was sitting out on the porch, and he just stopped to see; he wanted her name and everything. Aunt Sara was beautiful, she was one beautiful woman, and she had that gorgeous voice, and he just fell deeply in love with her.

I guess he sold Mil Nickels some fruit trees and Sara was actually selling china, some type of mail-order dishes, and A.P. bought all the dishes that he could afford, to try to put himself in good graces with Sara.

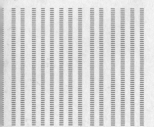

I GREW UP ON THE SIDE OF CLINCH MOUNTAIN,

WITH THE BEAUTIES AND THE MUSIC OF THE WOOD,

THE SWEET SONG OF THE BRIGHT, BUBBLING FOUNTAIN,

AND THE WARBLE OF THE BIRDS I UNDERSTOOD.

—A. P. CARTER, "IN THE SHADOW OF CLINCH MOUNTAIN," 1937

FERN SALYER: Music to them was everyday. They'd get on the front porch, and the neighbors would come and listen to 'em. We all grew up in it, and we thought, "Well, everybody does this, this is nothing new and different." Maybelle taught herself when she's six years old, I think. She couldn't even reach the guitar; she'd climb up on a chair.

Maybelle Carter, Sara Carter, and A. P. Carter

Sara Carter (banjo) and her cousin (autoharp)

MAYBELLE CARTER: I had a sister about the same age as [Sara], and I remember they used to play together quite a bit. One of them played the banjo and the other one played the auto-harp. The autoharp was the first thing that I ever played, then I played five-string banjo, and when I was thirteen years old, I started playing guitar. . . . No one showed me, I just figured it out myself.

SARA CARTER: Before Maybelle married, they used to live in Bristol, and she'd come down and visit me, and I'd go up there. She got to going with A.P.'s brother, and wasn't long until they were married, so she come to Poor Valley, too. She played the guitar and I played the harp. We'd get together and, you know, flump around on that, and sing. Maybe go to a neighbor's home once in a while. . . . It was just our natural way of playing—we didn't know any music, we just played by ear.

Me and A.P. first tried out for a [record] company. . . . I believe it was Brunswick. Just him and myself, when we were first starting. I don't remember what songs we sung, but anyway, they said there's no need for us people being poor people, the talent we had. They wanted to sign us up, but they didn't want to pay any royalties, so we wouldn't sign up. I think it might have been a year before this other come up. . . .

DALE JETT: As I understand it, A.P. saw an ad in a newspaper. . . . He found out that Ralph Peer and Victor recording machine company was coming to Bristol, was looking for artists to record. And, of course, A.P. was enthusiastic. Sara and Maybelle—I think family was first, and I know it would have been a difficult task to sell these women on that.

MAYBELLE CARTER: He came back home and he told us, he said, "There's a man from RCA Victor in Bristol, looking for talent to make records." And, of course, we didn't think anything about it. He got ready to go; he wanted Sara and I to go with him, you know, and—I've laughed about this several times since—so when we got ready to leave, I said, "Should I take my guitar?"

He said, "Why sure, we can't make a record without your guitar."

So we took off and went to Bristol.

DALE JETT: They left early one morning here, they had to ford the river, they forded creeks. . . . They were in a Model T, Model A, whatever, and with the tires back then, you were constantly fixing flats—you patched the tube and you pumped it up with the hand pump and went on your way.

FERN SALYER: There was muddy roads, they didn't even have gravel roads. . . . Aunt Maybelle was nine months pregnant with Helen, didn't feel very good, and every time she hit a bump she didn't know, you know—"Are we gonna have this baby out here or what?" But she went on, 'cause A.P. was very persistent. They didn't even have a car, he had to borrow his brother's—Maybelle's husband's—car to go, and I don't think he was real happy about that, either. And Sara had Joe, he was a baby, and they took [their older daughter] Gladys along to take care of Joe.

DALE JETT: Gladys, she told me she kept Joe outside when they were actually doing the recording—said she was trying to keep him quiet and occupied—and she said Bristol has never been as clean as it was that day, because she picked up every piece of paper, every rock and threw it in the creek for Joe—or gave it to Joe to throw in the creek—to keep him busy.

RALPH PEER: They wander in, they've come about twenty-five miles, and they've come through a lot of mud. . . . He's dressed in overalls, and the women are, you know, they're country women from way back there. Calico clothes on. Children are very poorly dressed. They looked like—well, later I called them "hillbillies," and that's what they looked like. . . . But as soon as I heard Sara's voice, that was it.

MAYBELLE CARTER: They just had an old building that we recorded in. It wasn't a regular studio, it was just an old warehouse. We did everything we did on one mike. They cut on a big wax, about so thick, and if you make a mistake you have to shave it off—you couldn't erase it like you do a tape, you know—had to start all over again. . . .

When we made the record and they played it back to us, I thought, "Well, it can't be!" You know, I just didn't have any idea of ever doing anything like that. . . . It just seemed so unreal, that you stand there and sing and then turn around and [they] play it back to you.

DALE JETT: They recorded four songs the first day, and the second day they recorded two songs. A.P. didn't return on the second day—he stayed in Bristol, but he didn't return in the studio to record—and Sara and Maybelle recorded "Wandering Boy" and "Single Girl, Married Girl."

SARA CARTER: I didn't want to sing "Single Girl, Married Girl." Mr. Peer had to beg me to sing that. I didn't like it. So, we made it, and when we got our first royalty check, why, that was the big one.

SINGLE GIRL, OH, SINGLE GIRL,

SHE GOES TO THE STORE AND BUYS . . .

MARRIED GIRL, OH, MARRIED GIRL,

SHE ROCKS THE CRADLE AND CRIES.

—A. P. CARTER, "SINGLE GIRL, MARRIED GIRL," 1927

Taylor-Christian Hat Company,
State Street, Bristol

Carter Family songbooks

SARA CARTER: It wasn't long after that until he called us back to make more records. . . . We went to New York, I think, for our next recording. We made several trips to New York, and we made some in Louisville, Kentucky, and Atlanta, Georgia; Charlotte, North Carolina—all different places.

DALE JETT: They paid them fifty dollars a song, supposedly, for everything that they brought in, and half a cent royalty a record. [It] was a very important amount of money, because this was in the Depression there, when people were literally starving. So I know the money was important to them at that time, but I think the songs themselves were, too.

FERN SALYER: A.P. had a dream, he wanted to do more. He would go out and walk for miles and stay gone for a week or two at a time; went from house to house in different communities looking for songs. He rescued them; they were gonna be gone, and he'd take them and go home and maybe rearrange them.

DALE JETT: It became almost a sickness, maybe. . . . Because I think to Sara and Maybelle, their children were the first thing in their lives—that was number one, and music was number two. In A.P.'s life, music was number one and family was number two, and that ultimately might have been his downfall.

BERNARD: The Carter Family are often portrayed as this very traditional, family-oriented group with very old-fashioned values. But when we actually began looking into the story, it was much more complicated. They were from these tiny mountain communities, but Maybelle's husband had a job with the postal service, so they lived in Washington for a while. And the romantic stories of A.P. rambling the mountains in search of songs also had a bit of a dark side: you listen to the interviews Sara did later, with her second husband, Coy Bayes, and realize she was left on her own with the children, and she had to work to support them. They talk about her "mining timber," going out to gather wood to sell to the mines and the railroads.

SARA CARTER: He mostly just roamed around through the country, just traveled around. . . . Sometimes he'd come in with a gang of chickens or geese, or a hog or something. He was just trading, trafficking around. I'd be with the horse, go up there myself, hauling timber out of the mountain, dragging them out. . . . That's when we was still living together.

FERN SALYER: He was gone a lot, she was home a lot, and she didn't really care that much about going after the music. She liked kinda being at home. So they just decided to split up. That was very unusual—I guess it was probably the first divorce that was ever in our family.

The Carter Family and children

SARA CARTER: I don't remember what year we separated in, to tell you the truth. Anyway, we worked together all the time after we separated. In fact, we got along better after separating. I went back over on Copper Creek and stayed there, but I'd come back and forth to rehearse when we got ready to go off to make a recording. We'd have to get together and rehearse our numbers, have them all timed out and ready.

MAYBELLE CARTER: We had an autoharp and a guitar, and that's all we had, so I had to do all of the lead on the guitar, and Sara just played background with the autoharp. Sometimes if I didn't have the key on the autoharp, I'd have to take a capo and fix another guitar for her to play in the key that I was in. And I used to try to play a little steel guitar—I just turned my strings down, put a little steel bar under the neck, and played on my regular guitar, you know. Anything to get something a little different.

SARA CARTER: About all [A.P.] done was just sing the bass. It was up to me and Maybelle to learn and arrange the music and everything.

MAYBELLE CARTER: This is what A.P. would do, when we was recording: if he felt like singing, he'd sing; and if he didn't, he'd walk over and look out the window. Anytime he took a notion, he'd just walk right off and look out, just same as nothing's going on. I remember Sara started a lot of times, "A.P., why don't you sing when you're supposed to?"

And he'd say, "Well, I'll get in there. Don't worry about me. I'll be there."

But I guess it made people take more notice to his singing, you know, listening to it closer. 'Cause everybody always has something to say about A.P.

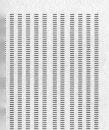

OH, BURY ME UNDER THE WEEPING WILLOW,

YES, UNDER THE WEEPING WILLOW TREE.

SO HE MAY KNOW WHERE I AM SLEEPING,

AND PERHAPS HE WILL WEEP FOR ME.

—A. P. CARTER, "BURY ME UNDER THE WEEPING WILLOW," 1927

BERNARD: Ralph Peer was a song publisher, and when he talked about the Carter Family he was very clear that they were valuable to him in a large part because they had this wealth of material that had not been published elsewhere—not necessarily songs they had written themselves, but at least unfamiliar songs that they collected and adapted, which he could publish. After Sara's voice, that was the great thing about them: the incredible breadth of their repertoire.

SARA CARTER: As long as we was making records, we had to get out and find material. They didn't want us to put anything on there that had been used or copyrighted or anything. When we was out giving personal shows, we'd gather up a lot of material that way. We'd maybe go spend the night with somebody and they'd have songs and want us to record them.

MAYBELLE CARTER: We worked these little old schools, and sometimes churches, around close to home in Tennessee, Kentucky, and Virginia. We just had a few little handbills, that was about it. . . . We'd usually just take off side roads and everywhere and stick them up around, or leave them in stores or places like that, public places.

SARA CARTER: Sometimes they'd be large crowds—sometimes you couldn't all get in the building, and we had to do two or three shows at one place in order to get them all in. I don't remember what they charged—about twenty-five cents? I guess you'd call it pretty good money back then. . . .

A.P. done the announcing of the numbers. He'd mostly just get up and tell about our records, he'd maybe tell about the song. He liked to play in person. He just liked to travel around and to be in different places. [For me] it was just a business, to help out, you know. I didn't mind making records, that wasn't much of a job. [But] the road, no; that's a hard life.

BERNARD: Talking to Fern and Dale, and listening to the old interviews, we were struck by all the different ways one can tell the Carters' stories. There is this constant temptation to portray them as isolated, ancient characters from the hills, but they were also very modern in some ways. For example, when A.P. went out looking for songs, it seems that his most frequent companion was a black man named Lesley Riddle.

Lesley Riddle

DALE JETT: Lesley Riddle was from Burnsville, North Carolina, and he lived in Long Island, which is kind of a suburb of Kingsport, Tennessee, and he used to go on song-collecting trips with my grandfather. What I remember of him when I was a kid, he would come over, and he had a wooden leg. He had lost a leg in a train accident, and supposedly the Carter Family brought him his first wooden leg—you know, prosthetic. He was a small-framed guy, and where I grew up, you know, he was one of the first black people I ever seen.

In this area—you're in the South, and on the Jett side of my family they had slaves, fought for the South in the Civil War—a black and white relationship back in those days around here was pretty much unheard of. One story I heard is that A.P. and Lesley went somewhere on a song-collecting trip, and they went in a restaurant to eat and they wouldn't serve Lesley Riddle, and A.P. said, "Well, if you can't serve him, you can't serve me," so they both left. I thought that was pretty cool.

SARA CARTER: [Lesley] was always so crazy about our records. . . . He found us, and so he just come over and stayed with us. He'd stay for weeks at a time and help us all he could. He was a good guitarist, and he was a good singer. We learned a lot of songs from him. I think it was a lot of help to us, getting his way of playing. Of course, we'd change it to our way.

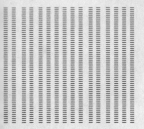

MY BABY LEFT ME, SHE EVEN TOOK MY SHOES,

ENOUGH TO GIVE ME THE DOGGONE WORRIED BLUES,

SHE'S GONE, SHE'S SOLID GONE.

—LESLEY RIDDLE, "CANNONBALL BLUES,"
AS SUNG BY THE CARTER FAMILY, 1937

BERNARD: We first came to the Carters through their records, but one of the other things that struck us about them is that they were involved in both of the main waves of America hearing itself for the first time. They made their first impact in that early wave of rural recordings, and then the next stage was the arrival of radio, and in the late 1930s they went to Texas and were on XERA, a border station based in Mexico that could be heard all over the central and western United States.

MAYBELLE CARTER: The first year we worked in Mexico in person, we had to go over there every night, and we were on for an hour from nine to ten. After that, we just started cutting transcriptions and sending them to the stations. [Those programs] used to be blasted all over the world. I never saw as much mail in my life—we'd get mail from every state in the Union.

BERNARD: It's curious, because there is that first love story of A.P. and Sara, and it seems very ancient and pastoral—him walking over the mountain and hearing this lovely voice in the distance. But in Texas, she kind of rang a modern technological change on that story: there was this fellow named Coy Bayes who she had been fond of in Virginia, but he had moved out to California and they'd lost touch, and then he heard her on one of the broadcasts from Mexico.

COY BAYES: One night, Dad and I were sitting there in the house, we had the radio on, and all at once the Carter Family bursted out over the radio. We ain't never dreamed of them being on the radio. . . .

SARA CARTER: You got to listenin' in every night.

COY BAYES: Yeah, naturally. They were calling the mail to Chicago, and I set down and I wrote Sara a card. So then in turn, I got a card from her, and we started writing. She told me she was divorced from A.P. and all. And of course, all through the years, I hadn't married. And we just made up our mind I guess to get married. . . . A.P., of course, he hit the ceiling. . . .

SARA CARTER: No, he didn't want me to marry nobody.

COY BAYES: He felt as if she was kind of dedicated to him in a way, or something. He didn't understand that Sara had her own life to live. He just thought, well, if he couldn't keep her or have her, why nobody else—

The Carter Family in Mexico with radio station XERA

SARA CARTER: —had no business with me.

COY BAYES: Maybelle's children were growing up and they were growing into an act of their own, and I knew that it was falling apart anyway. So I said, "Let's go back to California and settle down. I think we will be a little happier." And that's just what happened.

DALE JETT: I think my grandfather was brokenhearted, because he worshipped her, I really believe, from the time that he first heard her singing "Engine 143" in that holler across the mountain. I don't think he ever lost that love, and it was sad.

FERN SALYER: Maybelle went with her girls, and they played in Richmond, they played in North Carolina, they played in Knoxville, and that's where they hooked up with Chet Atkins. They got asked to go to the Grand Ole Opry, and [the Opry] said, "We don't want Chet Atkins, we just [want] you-all." But they wouldn't go without him, so they finally went together. And Elvis Presley toured with them for a while. He wasn't that big at that time, and Aunt Maybelle said she couldn't keep the buttons sewed on his jacket where he was jumping around.

A.P. missed that, being in the show business—he didn't just lose his wife, he lost his showmanship and getting onstage and doing things. . . .

A. P. Carter, 1950s

DALE JETT: Maybelle, she's seen the fruits of her labor, more so, as opposed to A.P. I've got a piece of paper showing he borrowed twenty-five dollars from the bank in 1959, the year before he died. And I can tell you, he didn't drink, he didn't squander it away. But I'm not sure that he ever really wanted a whole lot. Really, he wanted to make music, that was his passion.

He opened a little grocery store, and he also stayed down here at the Hilton fire tower, on top of Clinch Mountain—there's a watchtower that the forestry department would pay someone to stay up in the tower and watch for forest fires, and he worked up in the fire tower in the late

'50s, not too long before he died. That's kinda odd to me, too—you know, it would be very lonely. . . . But, there again, it would have been peace and quiet, and maybe he still had songs left in his head.

FERN SALYER: Well, you know, [Bob] Dylan, he asked Johnny Cash once, he said, "Johnny, did you ever meet A.P. Carter?" And Johnny said, "No, I never had that opportunity. . . . I didn't know him." And then he said, "But I guess nobody knew him." And it's kinda like that: nobody knew A. P. Carter.

*Elder Burch with his wife, Effie (lef
and daughter, Cora (righ*

4 | MY HEART KEEPS SINGING:
ELDER J. E. BURCH

Reverend F. W. McGee

BERNARD: When we began the *American Epic* project I knew I wanted to devote a major section of it to gospel music. Most of the people who listen to early blues and country music today are much less interested in the religious music that came out of the same communities, but when we were talking with musicians, they almost always mentioned church music, and many of them also sang Christian songs. The Carter Family made a lot of gospel records, and bluesmen like Charley Patton often had simultaneous careers recording religious songs—usually under pseudonyms, since church people tended to frown on blues. In the African American community, gospel music has had an enormous influence on secular styles and been the training ground for many of the most popular stars, from people like Aretha Franklin and James Brown up to Beyoncé.

In the 1920s, some of the most popular records among African American consumers were of preachers who mixed sermons with singing by their congregations. Reverend J. M. Gates was the most famous, but there were many others, such as the Reverend F. W. McGee. They were unbelievably influential, in terms of speaking to people and influencing the community—much more influential than the blues singers were. But if you want to learn about those figures, there has been very little research even on the biggest stars.

When I began looking for recordings to include in this project, I listened to dozens of records, and I was particularly struck by one called "My Heart Keeps Singing," billed on the label in gold lettering as a "sermon with orchestra" by "Elder J. H. Burch." The song itself is quite slow and simple, but the fact that the choir is singing a cappella—without any instrumentation—makes it very powerful. It conveys a sense of people leaving their worldly concerns behind and reaching a higher plane—the singers sound transported, and they transport the listener as well.

RACE RECORDS.
Records by:

Address-- Cheeraw,
South Carolina.

BURCH. (Elder J.E. & Congregation.)

007 0670 I

Marking	Letter	Pitch	Serial Number	Matrix Number	SELECTION. COMPOSER, PUBLISHER, ETC.	Wax	Rec.	F. Cur.	Amp. Set	Level	F. I.
			Inst--		Atlanta Georgia,Oct.23rd.1927.#51 S.Forsyth.St.3rd.Floor. Guitar,Tamberine, Snare Drum, Bass Drum.						
M	BVE	100	40338	1	God's Dwelling Place.	55-387R	124	9	9-4	46	0
H/	BVE	100	40338	2	Comp.J.E.Burch. Pub. & Copyr.R.S.Peer.1927.	55-390R	"	"	9-4	46	0
H/	BVE	100	40339	1	Baptism By Water And Baptism By	55-312	"	"	9-4	46	0
M	BVE	100	40339	2	The Holy Ghost. Comp. Burch. Pub. & Copyr.R.S.Peer.1927.	55-387	"	"	9-4	46	0
H/	BVE	100	40340	1	Will You Obey God.	55-383	"	"	9-3	44	0
M	BVE	100	40340	2	Comp.Burch. Pub. & Copyr.R.S.Peer.1927.	55-388	"	"	9-4	46	0
M	BVE	100	40341	1	The Church And The Kingdom.	55-387	"	"	9-3	44	0
H/	BVE	100	40341	2	Comp.Burch. Pub. & Copyr.R.S.Peer.1927.	55-390R	"	"	9-4	46	0
H/	BVE	100	40342	1	Wash You, Make You Clean.	55-391R	"	"	9-3	44	0
M	BVE	100	40342.	2	Comp.Burch. Pub. & Copyr.R.S.Peer.1927.	55-391	"	"	9-4	46	0
H/	BVE	100	40343	1	Life And Death.	391391	"	"	9-3	44	0
M	BVE	100	40343	2	Comp.Burch. Pub. & Copyr.R.S.Peer.1927.	55-381	"	"	9-4	46	0
H/	BVE	100	40344	1	The Prayer Service.	55-381	"	"	9-3	44	0
M	BVE	100	40344	2	Comp.Burch. Pub. & Copyr.R.S.Peer.1927.	55-383	"	"	9-4	46	0
H/	BVE	100	40345.	1	Love Is My Wonderful Song.	55-383	"	"	9-3	44	0
M	BVE	100	40345	2	Comp.Burch. Pub. & Copyr.R.S.Peer.1927.	550383	"	"	9-4	46	0
H/	BVE	100	40346	1	My Heart Keeps Singing.	55-381R	"	"	9-3	44	0
M	BVE	100	40346	2	Comp.Burch. Pub. & Copyr.R.S.Peer.1927.	55-346	"	"	9-4	46	0
					Time 11.00 To 3.15 P.M.						

Ralph Peer's recording log from the Elder Burch session

EVER SINCE MY SINS [EVER SINCE MY SINS] BEEN TAKEN AWAY [BEEN TAKEN AWAY],

MY HEART KEEPS SINGING, SINGING, SINGING ALL THE TIME.

SINCE JESUS WASHED [SINCE JESUS WASHED] ME IN HIS BLOOD [ME IN HIS BLOOD],

MY HEART KEEPS SINGING, SINGING, SINGING ALL THE TIME.

I'M SANCTIFIED [I'M SANCTIFIED] WITH THE HOLY GHOST [WITH THE HOLY GHOST].

MY HEART KEEPS SINGING, SINGING, SINGING ALL THE TIME.

SINCE JESUS WASHED [SINCE JESUS WASHED] ME IN HIS BLOOD [ME IN HIS BLOOD],

MY HEART KEEPS SINGING, SINGING, SINGING ALL THE TIME.

—ELDER J. E. BURCH AND CONGREGATION, "MY
HEART KEEPS SINGING," 1927

BERNARD: I was transfixed, and immediately knew I wanted to include this record. So I went looking for information about Elder Burch, and what I found could have been written on the inside of a matchbook: on Sunday, October 23, 1927, he and some members of his congregation recorded nine sides in Atlanta. That was it. Outside of that one recording session, Elder Burch was a complete mystery.

Fortunately, many of the original Victor recording sheets have survived and are archived in the basement of the Sony Records building in New York. These were typewritten sheets that the recording engineers would keep for each session, documenting when and where the recording took place, the names of the musicians, and how to identify the master discs. They went from the turn of the century up into the 1970s, with everyone from Enrico Caruso to Elvis Presley, and in the "B" section I found the sheet for Elder J. E. Burch. The initials were different, but the list of titles included "My Heart Keeps Singing." The only other information was the group's home location, which was given as "Cheeraw, South Carolina."

51 South Forsyth Street, Atlanta, Georgia, site of the Elder Burch recording session

The spelling was a bit off, but we found a Cheraw, South Carolina, billed on its website as "the prettiest town in Dixie." I telephoned the library there, and they had no information on Elder Burch, but suggested I contact Sarah Spruill, the town historian. She was the wife of a local judge, and answered the phone in a fantastically genteel voice, as if she had just stepped out of a garden party at Tara. She was intrigued by the Burch mystery, but hadn't heard the name—she suggested I talk to Felicia Flemming-McCall, who ran a museum of African American history. By now we were sufficiently intrigued that we decided to go to Cheraw.

ALLISON: It really was a lovely place, with magnolia trees lining the streets and beautiful white colonial houses. It felt like we were going back in time. We only planned to visit for a couple of days, but that turned into a week. Felicia Flemming-McCall hadn't heard of Elder Burch, but she said, "If anyone would know about him, it's Ted Bradley," and she gave us di-

Elder Burch's boarding house, Cheraw, South Carolina

rections to his home. We drove literally across the tracks to the old African American neighborhood, and we came to this modest little home up on a hill. Ted came out to welcome us, and he was one of the warmest people we met during this whole project, with a beatific smile, and he invited us inside. And as soon as we mentioned Elder Burch, he just lit up—it was like we were bringing back memories he hadn't thought about in seventy years.

TED BRADLEY: I was born three miles from Cheraw, in a place called Wilson Hill, and then my mom moved back from Wilson Hill to Cheraw—we moved to Front Street—and here I am today, eighty-four years old, and I am just grateful that I have the opportunity to share the story about Elder Burch, a man I admired when I was seven, eight years old. I never heard him preach, but every kid on Front Street knew Elder Burch. . . .

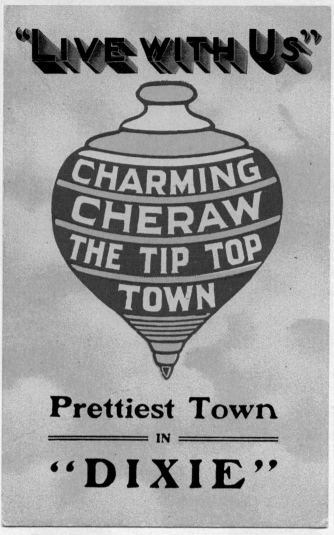

"LIVE WITH US"

CHARMING CHERAW THE TIP TOP TOWN

Prettiest Town IN "DIXIE"

He had a little store on the corner of Church and Second Street, and we'd walk up to this corner on a Saturday afternoon or a Sunday after church, and back in the day they had these old refrigerators with these large ice cubes in them, and he would fill those things up with Kool-Aid and stick a stick in them, and we called them Popsicles. There were two kinds, red and grape, and we would go out on a Sunday and pick up bottles and sell them for a penny and get a Popsicle—by the time you got back to the railroad track it was all melted, you had to run get another one. He sold five cookies for a penny, or you could get a pack of candy with ten pieces in it for a penny.

Other than that, he had a café, he had tables and chairs where the grown-ups could come and eat, and he served such meals as stew meat and rice, neck bones and rice, for fifteen cents

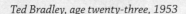
Ted Bradley, age twenty-three, 1953

Elder Burch, early 1900s

a plate. And he had a boardinghouse—that was during segregation, and if a black was coming through Cheraw they couldn't stay at the motel, so he provided rooms in his hotel there. I think he had about three rooms upstairs and about three or four downstairs. And on the front side of the corner was a barbershop—to tell the truth, Elder Burch had a whole little town of his own right there on that corner.

I can remember so vividly: he would stand out in front, and he would put his hands behind his back and stand there, kind of rocking, and people would gather around and he would be talking to them. He had salt-and-pepper hair, and he always wore nice clothes, vests and gold chains, you know, and whatnot. He had a yellow complexion, hair was always nice; he had a watch and rings on his fingers. . . . We would come up: "Elder Burch, you got any Popsicles today?"

Elder Burch in his restaurant with his daughter and wife, circa 1920s

"Yeah, come on in."

And I would stand there and look at his shoes: he had those fine shoes on, they looked so soft. . . . He would ask questions like where you lived, who our parents were. He would want to know all of that. "Do you go to church?" "Did you go to Sunday school?" He had a wonderful talk, he knew what to say and how to express himself in words. . . . I was so amazed at his fine suit, his complexion, and how he could talk, you know, and I always wanted to *be* like him. That's why I can tell you about it so well today.

There's very few people now who know anything about Elder Burch, very few people. The people who're on the far-end side of town didn't come on this side of town—they knew he was preaching at Triumph Church, but they never bothered to come over to the store, nothing of that nature. From Front Street, from Kershaw Road, these were the people who patronized

SECTION NO. I — THE INTERNATIONAL RELIGIOUS CONGRESS of TRIUMPH, THE
BEGINNING JULY 20-1

his store there, and some of those members from out at Triumph Church, they knew where he was. But the people over at the Presbyterians and the Methodists, they didn't bother to patronize him.

In the Holiness field, which is Triumph, it's a Sanctified church. When I say "Sanctified churches," they are more or less like—have you heard of Holy Roller? Well, it was more of that type church, where you would speak in tongues and roll around, and shout around, and dance around, and stir around. . . . It was the kind of church that they just praised the Lord—any way, any form or fashion, whatever it took, that's what they did, you know? If it meant rolling around on that floor in there and kicking up your heels and stomping, that's what they did. The Presbyterian and Methodist style, it was a little bit above that "down-home," that "junkyard music," we called it. You had these schoolteachers and these little businessmen, they knew what was happening at the Triumph, but they wouldn't participate. That was just a little bit too much for them, so to speak. They would maybe come, but sit out in their cars and listen. . . .

Triumph had a unique sound: they made music with tambourines and the heel of their shoe, and a big bass drum. It was a wooden church and it was built on kind of stilts like, and that stomping would go out the bottom of that church and you could hear it keeping time with the music that was playing in the church. That stomp was nothing but their heels on the wooden floor, and you could hear that stomp along with that old drumhead—*Boom! Boom!*— and tambourines, and an old rubboard, a rubbing board, you know, to wash clothes with.

and KINGDOM of GOD in CHRIST. LASTING FIFTY DAYS
R. E. D. SMITH, APOSTLE

BERNARD: Ted said there was another man I should speak with, Ernest Gillespie, who was around the same age and might be able to tell me more. He lived in Flushing, New York, and had actually written a little self-published book about his life in Cheraw. I went to see him, and he remembered Triumph Church fondly—though he also recalled the other churches looking down on it.

rnest Gillespie, age nine, 1936

ERNEST GILLESPIE: First of all, the ministers who were there did not go to seminary and learn to be ministers; they were people that said God called them to preach. They knew the Bible, they could read—because during that time there were many people who couldn't read, as my grandmother who was a slave could not read—and he would read the Bible and interpret what he thought it meant and he would preach on that. And also he would speak in tongues; sometimes he would talk for a minute or two and no one knew what the hell he was saying, because it was not a language, really—they say God understands it, but *we* don't understand it. And whenever he would speak in tongues, that was when the church would go completely crazy. . . .

I was Presbyterian and we had a Sunday service, but our

service was early, and when that service was over we would come over to Triumph. Our parents didn't know where we were, because most of our parents didn't want us to come over here to a Sanctified church, but we would come anyway, and generally when we got there we would have to stand in the back of the church, because it was just full of people all the time. . . . We were afraid to clap our hands and pat our feet because someone would see us there that might tell our parents. So we just stayed quietly in the back and listened to the music.

I'M GONNA PREACH SO GOD CAN USE ME, RIGHT DOWN HERE IN THIS WORLD.

I'M GONNA PREACH SO GOD CAN USE ME, RIGHT DOWN HERE IN THIS WORLD.

I'M GONNA SING SO GOD CAN USE ME, RIGHT DOWN HERE IN THIS WORLD.

I'M GONNA SING SO GOD CAN USE ME, RIGHT DOWN HERE IN THIS WORLD.

—ELDER J. E. BURCH AND CONGREGATION,
"THE PRAYER SERVICE," 1927

BERNARD: That first conversation with Ernest Gillespie included a rather startling revelation: He was telling me these stories, and then suddenly, out of the blue, he said, "You know, Dizzy used to go to that church."

"Dizzy?" I asked.

"Dizzy Gillespie," Ernest said. "He was my second cousin." And then he read me a passage from Dizzy's autobiography, *To Be or Not to Bop*. It turned out someone had written about Elder Burch and his music—it just wasn't a gospel historian.

DIZZY GILLESPIE: Like most black musicians, much of my early inspiration, especially with rhythm and harmonies, came from the church. Not my church though. In the Methodist church there wasn't too much happening musically—mostly hymns. But the Sanctified church had a deep significance for me, musically. I first learned the meaning of rhythm there and all about how music could transport people spiritually. The Sanctified church stood down the street from us, down near the end of the street, right near the place where we used to draw

Elder Burch with his wife, Effie (left), *and daughter, Cora* (right), *and his sons, Willie, John, and Joseph* (back row)

water from the well. The leader of the church was named Elder Burch, and he had several sons, Willie and Johnny Burch were two of them. . . .

Johnny Burch played the snare drum, and his brother Willie beat the cymbal; another one of the Burch brothers played the bass drum and the other the tambourine. They used to keep at least four different rhythms going, and as the congregation joined in, the number of rhythms would increase with foot stomping, hand clapping, and people catching the spirit and jumping up and down on the wooden floor, which also resounded like a drum. . . . Even white people would come and sit outside in their cars just to listen to the people getting the spirit inside. Everybody would be shouting and fainting and stomping. They used to shout awhile. The Sanctified church's rhythm got to me as it did to anyone else who came near the place. People like James Brown and Aretha Franklin owe everything to that Sanctified beat. I received my first experience with rhythm and spiritual transport going down there to the well every Sunday, and I've just followed it ever since.

TED BRADLEY: That water well right down below Triumph Church was a spring. They named it Buck Spring, I believe. But the whites owned that and they took that well and they made a pool, a swimming pool. You could stand in Triumph's backyard and you could see the pool, but you couldn't go to it, blacks couldn't go to it. Now listen to this: it was sitting that close to the black community—because that whole Huger Street there, where Triumph Church was, was all black, every house along there—and that pool was right there, and we couldn't go and swim in it. We could stand in the back of the church and throw a rock in the pool, but you couldn't go there.

Triumph, it sits on the edge of a white community; the only thing to separate 'em was a dirt road that separated the church from the white community. . . . You could spit across the street, it was white. When they were having the service and they'd get to playing and singing in there, the white folks, they would hear this, and they would come around. The church had all these windows on each side, and you could hear it going on, and there was some of the younger whites, they would get in the cars and drive around and park kind of at a distance so they could really hear what was going on.

ERNEST GILLESPIE: The street that I lived on in Cheraw—on the side of the street I lived on, there were all black families and across the street from us there were all white families. After five o'clock, when the people would come home from work, all the people from across the street would come out on their front porch in a chair with their guitars, play music, and sing hillbilly songs. They would do that until it got dark. We got so tired of hearing that hillbilly music, we didn't know what to do. Then they had a couple of radios, and when they weren't singing hillbilly music, they had it playing on the radio. And we discovered that if we went into our house, loosened a lightbulb and shook the bulb in the socket, it would cause static on their radios across the street. We would do this every afternoon until they finally stopped turning their radios on.

BERNARD: The old Triumph Church has been torn down, but a new church has been erected just a few yards away, and we were warmly welcomed by the current pastor, Elder Donnie Chapman. The church was small, simple, and unadorned, with chunky air-conditioning units struggling to counter the summer heat. In Elder Chapman's office, Allison immediately noticed an intriguing picture on the wall at the far end of the room. It was an oval-shaped painted portrait of a thoughtful-looking black man in a white collar and blue jacket, with a gold, five-pointed star on his left lapel, and at the bottom it said "Elder E. D. Smith." He was the founder of the Triumph Church movement, and there was an inscription below his name:

ELDER E. D. SMITH

Prophet, Bishop, Apostle, President and King of Triumph, the Church and Kingdom of God in Christ in North and South America. I was called of God to this work of Christ's kingdom October 20, 1897. He gave me the church January 20, 1902. May 7, 1915, He gave me the kingdom. He told me November 23, 1918, to go and tell the white people to loose the black people and let them go, for He has need for them. . . .

It sent shivers up our spines, this idea that in 1918 the Creator Himself had instructed Elder Smith to tell the white people of the land to unshackle their black brothers. With almost a century of hindsight, it seemed like a prophecy of the role the black church would play in the civil rights movement, a promise of future leaders like Martin Luther King Jr., and a reminder of the deep roots of his message in thousands of small churches across the South. We had been attracted to Elder Burch by his music, but clearly there was another message here as well.

The subject in which we will use at this time will be found in Daniel, the seventh chapter and the twenty-seventh verse [Amen! Praise God!]: The church and kingdom. We are now representing a church and kingdom [Yes, Lord!]. John saw the church coming down from God out of heaven [Yes, sir!]. . . . That church is a clean church [Yes, Lord!], without spot or wrinkle. It's not a stone structure built somewhere, but it's a body of baptized believers [Oh yes!], believing in God. For that cause John saw it coming down [Jesus!] from God out of heaven. He saw a clean spirit coming in man, bless his great name. Then brother Daniel saw the kingdom, and he said, "The kingdom, and the dominion, and the greatness of the kingdom under the whole heavens shall be given to the people of the saints of the most high. [Yeah, Lord!] Bless his great name. . . . Jesus Christ is gonna reign king right in the earth! And every man, and every person that will obey God will have a share in that kingdom, hallelujah!

—ELDER J. E. BURCH AND CONGREGATION,
"THE CHURCH AND THE KINGDOM," 1927

Elder J. E. Burch with his wife, Effie

TED BRADLEY: That's where the leadership came from. It came from the preacher. . . . Every preacher came with the same message. And that message was "You're being depressed down, you're being pressed back or pushed back. And so you don't have to accept this, you need to do something about this." These preachers led the charge; they didn't stand back and let somebody else do it, they led the charge. . . .

Those songs lifted us up, those songs that we sang as a black race of people, like "Amazing Grace" and "Does Jesus Care?" "Be Not Dismayed." We'd sing those songs to get relief from the burdens of the day, from picking cotton, from cropping tobacco, from all of those hard tasks; those songs would relieve us from that hard day-work. When you heard one singing a song across the field, the whole field would take it up. It would go across the field just like a wave. . . . They

Painting of Burch Barbershop by Eleanor Spruill

would hear it going across there: *A-a-ama-a-zi-i-ing graaaace* . . . Then you'd hear 'em pick up on it, it was like, *Ho-ow-ow swee-eeet* . . . Then, after they sang it, they'd hum. And that just makes you forget about that hot sun on your back, down on your knees in that eighty-five-degree weather, picking that cotton. That was your way out.

ALLISON: We were so caught up in this story that we wanted to know more, but the memories of Elder Burch all ended sometime in the 1940s. No one in Cheraw could remember when he left town, or why, or where he might have gone. We were on the verge of giving up, but on our last night in town, with a plane flight scheduled the next morning, we went to a local rib shack for a farewell dinner and happened to mention to the owner why we had come to Cheraw. She went back to the kitchen, and when she came out with our food she handed us a cell phone and said, "Talk to this man." That was Evan Fuller, and as soon as he got on the phone, he told us, "I remember Burch! He went to Vineland, New Jersey."

Bernard did a bit of research and found that there was still a Triumph Church listed in Vineland, which is a small town in the southern part of New Jersey. So we drove down from New York, and that turned into another quest: we arrived in the evening and went to the address, and it was just an empty lot. You could tell something had been there once, but it was long gone. We were really disheartened, but we had already booked a hotel room, so we decided to stay the night. As we were walking down the main street we passed a fire station, and it occurred to me to ask them if they knew of any families named Burch. The fire chief said he was pretty sure there were, and told us the part of town he thought they were, and coincidentally it was very near the area where the church was supposed to be. So the next morning we went over there again, and as we were driving up, we saw a church with this big orange cross on the top. We were ecstatic, sure that we'd finally found it, but when we got to the door it was some kind of Episcopal church. Our hearts sank. But then, right beside it, set back off the road, we spotted a humble little house with a peeling sign saying "Triumph Church." We couldn't believe it. We had finally found it.

We ran over, wondering what to do next, and almost immediately a car pulled up with four people in it. That turned out to be the whole congregation, coming for their weekly service. They were a bit hesitant to talk to us at first, but then the elderly lady who was the leader said she remembered Elder Burch, who had founded the church—but it seems there had been some sort of split, and she did not care to tell us anything more about it.

At least we knew we were on the right track, so we decided to drive around and ask people if they knew anyone named Burch. It was a nice day, and there was a man out raking leaves, and we asked him, but he didn't know, and then we saw another man working in a yard, and Bernard went over to see if he could help. I was surprised when, after a few minutes of chatting, Bernard went and sat with the man on the stoop of his house and they stayed there chatting for over twenty minutes. I was sure it was just someone who wanted company and a bit of a chat so I stayed in the car and waited, but it turned out that his name was Bob Burch, and Elder J. E. Burch was his great-uncle, though he didn't know a lot about him. However, we were thrilled, because we had finally found a relative of Elder Burch after a two-year quest!

BERNARD: We still had not found anyone who knew what had happened to Elder Burch, but that gave us hope, so I contacted a professional genealogist who had access to sealed records for New Jersey, and eventually he tracked down another relative, a great-niece named Jackie Knaff, in Pittsburgh. So I called her, and she said, "You've come to the right place. Elder Burch's daughter, Cora, was my great-aunt, and she gave me all the family photographs, and I have a giant framed mural of pictures of him mounted on my mantelpiece."

She was kind enough to make us copies and, finally, we could see Elder Burch. He was exactly as Ted Bradley had described him: a light-skinned man, perfectly groomed, with the gold

Elder Burch

chain across his waistcoat and a penetrating stare that even in the photograph projected a sense of power. It was as if the final piece had fallen into place: we had been captivated by a voice on a rare record from the 1920s; had gone in search of the man himself, walking the streets he walked and conversing with people who had known him; and had followed his trail out of Cheraw and found his surviving family. Now, when we listen to that record again, it feels not like a mysterious voice from the distant past, but rather like the voice of someone we know, with a face and a community, connected to a familiar place.

We went back to Cheraw one more time, for a gathering of Triumph Church members in honor of J. E. Burch. Ted Bradley was there, and Ernest Gillespie. The minister preached, the choir sang, the congregation stomped, shouted, and got happy. It was a long journey, but for us at least, it felt as if Elder Burch had come home.

*Duke Erikson, Peter Henderson, Bernard MacMahon,
and Jack McLean after filming at the Triumph Church*

OKeh ELECTRIC

REG. U. S. PAT. OFF. MARCA IND.

RGTRADA NUM 22081 DE 22 DE MAYO DE 1923 M. R.

OKeh

ELECTRIC

REG. U.S. PAT. OFE MARCA IND. RGTRADA NUM 22081 DE 22 DE MAYO DE 1923. M.B.

FOR BEST RESULTS
USE OKeh NEEDLES

45127

Vocal
With Instrumental

**GONNA DIE WITH MY HAMMER
IN MY HAND**

WILLIAMSON BROTHERS
AND CURRY

(80757)

MADE AND PAT'D IN U.S.A. JAN. 21, '13 AND MAY 22-23
© OKEH PHONOGRAPH CORPORATION, NEW YORK

OKeh Needles

Truetone Needles

For Better Music Use These Needles

Okeh Phonograph Corporation

New York

5 GONNA DIE WITH MY HAMMER IN MY HAND:
DICK JUSTICE AND THE WILLIAMSON BROTHERS

Dick Justice medallion, 1929

BERNARD: One of my introductions to the music of this era arrived when I found an old sec-ondhand copy of the *Anthology of American Folk Music* album set in a bookstore in Streatham—all three volumes, bound in these Victoriana red cloth covers—and they were very important records for me as a teenager. The music was so raw and exciting, almost like punk, and one of my favorite tracks was "Henry Lee" by Dick Justice. It's an old Scottish ballad, but the way he did it was completely distinctive, and there was something about his voice that attracted me in a very powerful way. It was eerie and beautiful, and sounded like it was coming out of some really deep place, like a dark tunnel. The song itself was also very striking—it was actually a hit in the UK for Nick Cave and PJ Harvey in the 1990s, and their version was based on Dick Justice's. It's a murder ballad, like a lot of the ballads you find in the Appalachians, but a bit unusual because most of those songs are about men killing their girlfriends, but in this one the woman kills the man.

SHE LEANED HERSELF AGAINST A FENCE, JUST FOR A KISS OR TWO.

WITH A LITTLE PENKNIFE HELD IN HER HAND, SHE PLUGGED HIM THROUGH AND THROUGH.

COME ALL YOU LADIES IN THE TOWN, A SECRET FOR ME KEEP,

WITH A DIAMOND RING HELD ON MY HAND, I NEVER WILL FORSAKE.

—DICK JUSTICE, "HENRY LEE," 1929

Ervin Williamson

I was intrigued by this guy, and what made it particularly exciting was that I had absolutely nothing to go on but the music: I hadn't seen any pictures of him, I didn't know anything
about his story. This was before I began the *American Epic* project. I hadn't done any research,
and it somehow felt very personal: I wanted to establish a direct connection to this man, not
just burrow through libraries. The one thing I knew was that he was supposed to be from West
Virginia, and I knew that was a coal mining area, so I researched where some of the mining
centers were and started calling up editors of the local papers and asking if they would run

a short piece saying "British film company looking for relatives of Dick Justice." I contacted maybe five or six papers, and a couple of weeks later I called the editor of the *Logan Banner*, and he said, "We just ran your story, and an old man telephoned and left his number."

The man's name was Bill Williamson, and when I called him, he told me he knew Dick Justice's daughter, because he was a piano tuner and had tuned her piano. Her name was Ernestine Smith, and he gave me her number, and I thanked him, and then he said, "My father played with Dick Justice."

I said, "Really? Who is your father?"

He said, "Ervin Williamson. He made some records, too, as the Williamson Brothers and Curry."

That group had a track on the *Anthology* as well, a version of the John Henry ballad called "Gonna Die with My Hammer in My Hand," with this ferociously propulsive guitar and fiddle. Bill told me his father had worked with Dick Justice in the mines and had also played with Frank Hutchison—yet another artist from the *Anthology*. At that point I knew I had to go to Logan.

ALLISON: One of the things that is very noticeable as you cross America is how the landscape changes so dramatically from place to place. That contrast was particularly noticeable coming into Logan, because you leave the rolling countryside and it becomes more mountainous with interesting rock formations; the surface looks like black slate, and it actually reminded me of parts of the West of Scotland, where I'm from. Logan is a very small town, tucked in this valley between these steep, tree-covered hills, and as we approached there was a great black cloud hanging over it. It may have just been the time of year, but there was a feeling about it. The people we met there were wonderful—Ernestine Justice Smith and Bill Williamson, and we traveled up to Cleveland and talked with Ernestine's brother Eugene as well. But the landscape felt—I suppose the word I'm looking for is "menacing"—like life is harder there than it is in other places.

ERNESTINE JUSTICE SMITH: Dad came from a large family; he had four brothers and two sisters, as I recall. You see, things were really hard back then, and there was a saying, "If the coal miners are on strike, there's gonna be a lot of babies." There were a lot of strikes in the mines, so people had to get to doing other things when they couldn't work, if you know what I mean. It was so tough, my granddaddy took my dad out of school when he was eleven, and he had to go shoveling the coal in the mines. That was how poor they was.

Inside the Logan mines

EUGENE JUSTICE: From what I heard, when Dad first started working in the mine, it was only, like, maybe two or three foot [high], and he had to be on his hands and knees. He had to wear rubber knee pads. It was hard work—on your knees all day long, shoveling coal into a little carlike thing, fill the car up, and then they take the car out of the mines and bring it back in.

BILL WILLIAMSON: My grandfather on my dad's side, he by trade was a blacksmith, but he did work on the mining tip over at Shamrock, and that's how he met his death. He fell off the tipple and was killed. Back then, people had a hard way to go.

Dad, I think he went to the eighth grade—I remember they wanted him to go into teaching, because he was pretty intelligent, but he chose to have a family and to work in the coal mines and make money that way.

It was backbreaking work, long hours, and little pay. They went in the coal mine at daylight and they didn't get out until after dark. One story I remember my dad telling me: they hand-loaded coal with a shovel and they got paid fifty cents a carload, and they had what they called a "docking board." It was a board that the car had to go under, and if the coal wasn't high enough to drag the docking board, they would be docked for the whole car—in other words, they wouldn't get a dime out of it.

They took advantage of people back then, before the union. They worked people to death, they really did. There was a lot of mining accidents, and my dad told me, at that time, "Every time you go down in that mine you're just taking your life in your own hand." Now, later on in years, after the union came in, things were different then; they got paid. I can remember he made seventeen dollars a day—that's a lot of difference than getting paid fifty cents a coal car.

Ervin Williamson, Arnold Williamson,
Arnold Curry, and Kirk

EUGENE JUSTICE: I was raised in a mine company house. It was just a big square house, four rooms. We had electricity, but Mom cooked with an old coal stove. Had an old outhouse. You paid the rent to the coal company you worked for, they'd take it right out of your pay, and the electricity, all that came out of your pay. Give your money right back to the coal companies. They had their own little stores, right up there on Rum Creek where we lived. Most of the coal miners would go there and shop instead of downtown Logan; they'd end up spending all their money there and bringing nothing home.

BILL WILLIAMSON: The companies owned the houses the miners lived in, and paid them in what you call "scrip." It would have the coal company's name, and you could only use it in the company store. If you needed money to go somewhere else, you would have to sell the scrip for, like, sixty cents on the dollar. I remember when I was a child going through the streets of Logan, and on the restaurant windows they had a sign saying "We buy scrip," which means they would buy your scrip for sixty cents on the dollar. If you wanted a little bit of cash to spend in town, that's the only way you'd have it.

BERNARD: At some point in this project I coined a term, "geographonics," for the sense I often have that music is directly related to the place where it is created. Again and again, I've

had this feeling that I never really understood the music until I went where the musician lived. When I made my first trip to New York, I was in a yellow taxicab and [the driver] was playing Miles Davis's *Kind of Blue*, and of course I knew the record, but it had never made sense to me in the same way as it did hearing it in New York.

I had that feeling particularly strongly in Logan, listening to the music while driving through this deep gorge that's cut out of the mountainside. There's a kind of gritty, sharp edge to the Williamson Brothers' songs that sonically echoes that experience, like a pickax hitting coal. But the interesting thing is that the songs themselves don't particularly deal with that situation. I've found in the main that it's performers from more middle-class backgrounds, people like Bob Dylan or Woody Guthrie, who tend to affect that kind of persona, to sing about the hard life working in the mines. The people who are really from those environments, they rarely sing directly about that kind of thing.

One of the striking things about the Williamson Brothers is that they were in this very tough environment, working as miners or doing other jobs—Ervin Williamson apparently drove trucks and worked as a butcher, as well as spending twenty-seven years in the mines—and they never made a living from their music, but they seem to have had a very professional attitude about it. Bill Williamson is a piano tuner and technician who has worked for all sorts of famous artists, from the Dorsey Brothers and Guy Lombardo to Ronnie Milsap, and he constantly emphasized his father's perfectionism.

BILL WILLIAMSON: My dad played the piano and he helped me along to learn some, but any instrument he picked up had to be tuned perfectly or he wouldn't fool with it. He was particular, and if you didn't sit down with him and practice and get a song right, just don't sit down with him at all. He would go in the bedroom and play the banjo, and you could hear him just all by himself; he'd practice and practice and practice, because if he went out, he wanted to make sure that when he played music it was done the right way.

He played the piano, the guitar, five-string banjo, he played the accordion—he could play just about anything. And Uncle Arnold, he could play the guitar like Merle Travis—he had that technique and he was very good at that—but he played the piano and he played the violin, and he was good at all of them. And both of them was very, very particular. I'd go and tune up my uncle Arnold's piano for him, and he'd sit there by the side of me to make sure I did it right.

Uncle Arnold would bring the violin into our house on a Saturday evening, and they would play music all night on Saturday till daylight Sunday morning. And there was always a whole lot of people coming in our house to listen to the music, you know, because they were very, very

Ervin Williamson (banjo)
with his trio

good. I can remember it just like it was yesterday: everybody just sat around playing music, and if they wanted to get up and dance, let 'em dance. There was no booze, it was just good clean fun and good food; we always had good food for everybody.

Dad and Uncle Arnold were called the Williamson Brothers, and Arnold Curry was a cousin who traveled with them and played with them, too. They performed at square dances and things like that, and they had a good following—at that time you didn't have advertising or anything like that, but anytime someone heard where they was going to be, they would show up for the dance.

Dick Justice and Frank Hutchison, they were very good, and they all knew each other; they played music together many a time. When Dad made some recordings, Frank Hutchison helped him set up an audition, and they auditioned over the telephone, to the studio in St. Louis, Missouri. It was called OKeh, and they liked what they heard and they asked him to come on down.

Dad and Uncle Arnold and Arnold Curry and this other fella named Kirk, they went on down on a train. It was in 1927, and there was a big flood on the Mississippi River, and he told me he could look out the window of the train and all he could see was water, and see housetops sticking up out of the water. I don't know how they made it to St. Louis, but somehow they got there and they recorded six songs, and they got paid twenty-five dollars a song, and that was all, no royalties or anything, and that was it.

A lot of people has wondered why they didn't continue their career—I'm talking about, like, record collectors,

Frank Hutchison

and people like that—'cause they thought that they were good enough. But you didn't make that much money with it at that time, and they had family. Dad kept on playing: he would make these deliveries to what you call VFW clubs, the Veterans of Foreign Wars, and he would take and play the piano for them when he'd go in and make a delivery; they'd always make him go up and play some blues and boogie and stuff. And he enjoyed his life. He had a lot of heartache and hardships, but he enjoyed life, he really did.

I remember one song he used to do called "Cocaine," but it had a verse in it about the furniture man, so he liked to the call it "The Furniture Man," and he would just do it like a comedy skit, he'd just crack everybody up. There was one verse in it that says:

Furniture man came to my house early on Sunday morning,

Asked me was my wife at home, I said no,
she's long been gone.

Said he backed his wagon up to my door,
took everything I had,

Carried it all back to the furniture store and boy,
it made me feel bad.

BERNARD: For me, one of the most intriguing things about this period of recording is that, for every artist like a Carter Family or Memphis Jug Band that was very popular and made dozens or hundreds of records, there were a thousand other artists that we only know as a name on a record label. Their great moment, their great song, can be every bit as transcendent as anything the more famous artists recorded, and there is something very poignant and beautiful about that.

At the same time, one of the striking things about talking with people who knew those artists is that for them the records often seem to have been almost irrelevant, and the picture we get from the records doesn't always match what people remember. I was familiar with "Cocaine," but it was recorded by Dick Justice, not the Williamson Brothers. And it would never have occurred to me to associate any of the Logan players with boogie-woogie piano, but both Bill Williamson and Eugene Justice recall their fathers' piano playing. The weirdest thing was that I had traveled all the way to Logan because of Dick Justice's records, but Eugene said he had been unaware of the records and none of them sounded familiar.

EUGENE JUSTICE: When I first heard the recordings, I said, "Hell, that's not my dad." I didn't even know he had made any records until I was in my thirties. I know Dad sang, he played guitar, he played the piano, 'cause we had a piano at one time and he used to play it and sing. And in his last five to eight years, he joined the church and he would sing and play the piano—it sounded to me like a rock and roll song, you know, instead of something for the church—and them people *moved*. They loved it, man, I swear they did.

He was real quiet, never said much. That's one reason I guess I didn't know about him doing these recordings. Dad would work all week in the coal mines, and he would drink a little on the weekends, and that's the only time we would ever see him play anything. But I never heard him sing any of these songs he's supposed to have recorded. You know, "Henry Lee" is my brother's name, too—so he recorded this song, and when my brother came along, he gave him the name Henry Lee, but I never heard him sing it.

From what I hear, a guy named Pete Hell taught him how to play the guitar. He was a black guy, and I think he lived down around Wayne County—I believe that's where Dad learned to play the guitar. And he must have taught him pretty good, 'cause Dad could play real good. Every now and then they would have competitions on who could play the best, and Dad winned most of 'em. He played more like the blues type, and he'd play the piano, and I never did see him play a slide trombone, but he said he could.

AUG · 59

Dick Justice's baptism in the Guyandotte River, Logan, West Virginia

ERNESTINE SMITH: I suppose he would have loved to make a career out of music, but in those days it was hard to make a living and he had a family to feed. You see, my mother disapproved of his music. He used to enjoy a beer at weekends and that's when he'd play his songs; he would get together with his friends away from the house and they'd play together. He'd married very young, but his first wife died before they had any children, and he married my mother in 1933. She was very religious, so she didn't like him playing the guitar at all—it's a shame I can't tell you more about his music, but my mother didn't like him to talk about it.

ALLISON: That visit was strange for me. It was a feeling I had in so many towns during our travels, especially in the South. I don't know if it's just because of the huge chain stores and the Internet, but I noticed that many of the local shops are boarded up and empty. There's still mining there—it's very noticeable, because at regular intervals you see these long, long trains full of coal, and then you see them coming back again a while later, empty—but it's very obvious that what happens there is the mining industry and not much else. When you compare it with old postcards, you see that the buildings haven't changed, but that they're a lot more dilapidated and the businesses are gone.

BILL WILLIAMSON: Back many years ago there was so many coal miners, and all these coal camps and everything. People didn't have automobiles like they do now, so we had a bus company here in Logan and they ran buses up just every holler, and every Saturday the town would be so crowded you couldn't hardly walk up the street without turning sideways and dodging this one and dodging that one.

Of course, when they brought in automation a lot of these people got laid off. They have what they call continuous miners now, and the coal mine just sets up and you push buttons—I mean, there's more to that, obviously, but it's a lot different than coal miners going in with picks and shovels. When that come in, there were hundreds of coal miners put out of work, and they left and went to Ohio and Detroit and different places like that to find a job, because there weren't no work here for them.

EUGENE JUSTICE: I never was in a mine, except one time. Dad took me down in one, maybe two miles, and I didn't want no more. I said, "Get me back out of here." It's a eerie feeling, man, all that dirt over your head. Dad told me, said, "Son, don't ever go in there if you don't have to," and I took him at his word and I left. I come up here to Cleveland, and I been here ever since, working in a warehouse.

BILL WILLIAMSON: Dad retired when he was seventy-one, and he didn't live to see seventy-two, and he was buried on Easter Sunday of 1972. When he passed away he was having a lot of trouble with his breathing and everything; and, of course, he had already been approved for black lung. His lungs was hard, he couldn't breathe, you know. Of course, my dad's not the only one; that's the way it used to be. The regulations for the coal mines now, the coal companies try to fight 'em like crazy, but coal miners need to understand, the old-timers is what brought it as good as it is now.

Dad worked all his life—went from one job to another, but he was never without a job. The year that he died, he decided that winter not to work—he knew he was sick, and he wanted to take care of himself—but he was planning on going back to work in the spring. But he never did get well. But I'm telling you now, he was a tough man.

EUGENE JUSTICE: Dad died in '59. He didn't retire, he got hurt—I don't know exactly how; he hurt his knee some way. And then he got the cancer, you know, and passed away. We buried him up on a hill there—probably you'd never know it was there now, they grow it up so much. It's just weeds and trees.

Dick Justice outside his mine company house

DOWN THE DIRT ROAD: CHARLEY PATTON
AND THE MISSISSIPPI DELTA BLUES

Son House with girlfriend, circa 1929

BERNARD: Of all the environments that have given birth to unique styles of music, there is none more legendary than the Mississippi Delta. Our own journey into that world began back in Britain, and almost by chance. In 2006 my friend Garth Cartwright happened to notice a small mention in a specialist blues magazine that a festival in the Lake District was going to include Honeyboy Edwards, Homesick James, and Robert Lockwood Jr., three men in their nineties who had grown up at the height of the Delta blues era. This was before we had begun work on *American Epic*, but I could not pass up that opportunity, so we arranged to bring a crew to the country inn where they were staying, and filmed them talking about their youth and the music they had grown up with, including their memories of the formative genius of the Delta style, Charley Patton.

It was an amazing experience listening to these men who had lived through all the changes from the nineteenth to the twenty-first century, because the world they grew up in was still very much technologically in the nineteenth century, with no electricity or running water, and in a social and economic situation that was in many ways reminiscent of the old slave plantations. Watching them sitting together, trading stories and talking about the music and the Delta and how both had changed, and getting a sense of their outlook and the way they related to each other was a very profound experience.

When we began filming *American Epic*, our original plan was to build on that experience by bringing some of Patton's oldest surviving relatives back to Dockery Plantation, where they used to live. We made contact with the family, but it rather quickly became clear that the journey we had imagined did not make sense.

ALLISON: We got in touch with Kenny Cannon, who is Charley Patton's great-grandnephew, and his wife, Tracy, and they were very helpful and encouraging, and brought us to visit some

of the older relatives, who were living in Detroit. But when we would ask the older people to tell us what they remembered about the Delta, they'd say, "I don't remember anything." Some of that may have been because we were white outsiders, but there was also the fact that they did not have good memories of that time and place and didn't want to drag up the past. That was something Tracy and Kenny talked about as well, that for many African Americans this music is not connected with good memories, and they don't want to look back on that time. Fortunately, Kenny and Tracy themselves had been doing research on the family and were keen to visit Dockery with us, so we decided to make the trip with them and get that perspective: of young, modern people traveling back to the world of their grandparents.

It was a strange feeling driving down from Memphis through the Delta, because there is this incredible sense of emptiness. Part of it is just the atmosphere: most of that region used to be swampland, and the air was very thick and humid, and you have these magnificent skies with great, giant cumulus clouds, and this huge, flat, expansive landscape. But the other thing was that there seemed to be nobody there: we barely passed a car on the roads; there was nobody in the fields; there were just a few small churches dotted here and there. Especially in Dockery, which is really out in the country—it's miles from even the nearest small town—there is this sense of isolation. You can imagine how busy it would have been back in the day, when the plantation was full of workers and had its own railway spur to bring the cotton to market, but even in that time it must have felt quite isolated.

BERNARD: As always, we had a strong feeling that the music of Patton and his peers reflected the local geography, and I was struck by the extent to which that belief was already shared by people who were living in the Delta back then, when it was a center of musical innovation. Listening to interviews with H. C. Speir, who owned a furniture store in Jackson in the 1920s and was responsible for virtually all the recordings of early Delta blues, he clearly linked the music to its surroundings.

Group photo of Dockery workers

H. C. Speir

H. C. SPEIR: Flat country, you understand, bottoms and all that. That has a great effect on people, the way they sing. If you were sitting alone at night and heard an owl sing or blow or whistle—toot, that's what we call it—then it would make you kind of lonesome, you see. And whenever these Negroes, especially, when they would sing late in the evening, it was a lonesome sound, too.

There's something about when you're in what I call plantations, like, where there are groups of them and they sing in the evenings, you know, and at the time it gives them a spiritual uplift. . . . I tell you, that's a comfort to them, if they have been abused quite a bit. . . . And then, too, you got emotional setups, hard times, and echoes, and they'd be singing down into the bottoms and the swamps and so on like that. That gave them more incentive to put more into blues, you see.

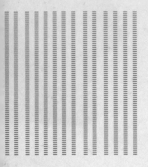

BACKWATER DONE ROSE ALL AROUND SUMNER NOW,
DROVE ME DOWN THE LINE,

BACKWATER DONE ROSE AT SUMNER, DROVE POOR
CHARLEY DOWN THE LINE,

LORD, I'LL TELL THE WORLD THE WATER, DONE COME
THROUGH THIS TOWN.

—CHARLEY PATTON, "HIGH WATER EVERYWHERE," 1929

TRACY CANNON: To come here to Dockery now is a very humbling experience: to know that [Kenny's grandmother], a woman that I know and love, as a child picked cotton on this plantation; to know that there were thousands of African Americans here on this plantation, enslaved against their will in the beginning, and then towards the end sharecropping for a meager existence. It puts it all into perspective.

HONEYBOY EDWARDS: Sharecropping means a white man has got a plantation; he's got money; he's got people on this plantation working for him. And everything, all the cotton you grow on the plantation, you had to give him half of it—it's on the halves: if you make twenty bales of cotton, he get ten, I get ten. But in the end of the year I got to pay him what I owe him out of my ten, and I ain't got nothing. Understand me? When I wind up, he got the ten I got and I've got to go back to him and get some more. That's the way the white man got over all the time. . . . There's been people moved from here and they go over there; get there, move from here and go there; kept a-moving, and they never did no better.

HOMESICK JAMES: I've been working at factories, steel mills; I was a dishwasher; I've been everything—railroad worker—to survive. . . . But my first job was a cotton field: "Catch that mule! Catch that mule and plow, boy!"

You know how to plow? Oh wait a minute, I'll teach you how: Somebody standin' over you with a bullwhip. Oh my God, yeah! You first, you got to chop it, then you got to grow it, then you pick it. Yeah. You got to take it to the gin, and then they gins it off. They got to suck the cotton out; they put the seeds in one place and the cotton goes in the other and they put it in bales. . . .

Didn't allow you to be involved with that money. The fact about it, it wasn't money; we used to get notes and stuff, you know? In my time, if you wanted some merchandise, if you want a pair of shoes—you working on the farm—well, he'd give you a note and then you'd take it to the merchant there, then he gave you the shoes. They wouldn't let you have no money. I think that it was maybe 1920 before I got my own money—'21, I seen a five-dollar bill and it scared me to death! I said, "I need some of these." That's the truth! I'm telling you guys this like it is. Until 1930, when I was nineteen years old, man, it was hard then. In '29, that's when I went up in Chicago there, and times was tough. It was hard there, too, but it was better than in the South.

KENNY CANNON: Music in that era, I guess, was a break from reality. You're sharecropping, you're working hard every day of your life, and it gives you an opportunity to get a break from that hard day-to-day work.

THERE'S A LITTLE BOLL WEEVIL, KEEP MOVING IN THE—LORDY—

YOU CAN PLANT YOUR COTTON AND YOU WON'T GET HALF A CENT, LORDY.

—CHARLEY PATTON, "MISSISSIPPI BO WEAVIL BLUES," 1929

HONEYBOY EDWARDS: I was born in Shaw, Mississippi, in 1915. My father played guitar and violin, my mother played harmonica. Back in them days you didn't have nothing but guitars, pianos, and violins, and mandolins and things—we made our own music, 'fore the electric music come out. That's why so many peoples [who] come from the South, they're playing the blues and different stuff like that. They learned their own music, 'cause they had to make it. That's where it come from.

Blues is like a story. You may say, "My baby left early this morning, which a-way did my baby go? Sometimes I wonder, I don't know." You know, stuff like that. There's different songs you can make. Like you make "Highway 61, it's the longest highway I know. It runs from New York City, clean to the Gulf of Mexico." And say, "When I die before my time, please turn my feet to the rising sun, and I'll be walkin' Highway 61." You got to put it together, you know? Make it sound—put it together, and rhyme it together.

KENNY CANNON: Charley Patton was my great-grandmother Viola Cannon's brother, and my grandfather John Cannon was raised on this plantation, with his siblings. They worked here and they were sharecroppers here. My grandfather's father, John Cannon Sr., he ran the grocery store here. My grandfather told me when I was young, probably seven or eight years old, he told me that I had a very famous uncle that sang blues. Actually, he said I have a very famous uncle who *invented* blues. That was just a story that kind of went through our family, that he invented blues, that he invented music, essentially.

HONEYBOY EDWARDS: I met Charley Patton in Ruleville, Mississippi, in '31. He lived on Dockery Plantation, about three miles from Ruleville and about five or six miles from Cleveland, betwixt each town. They called him the founder of the Delta—he was a good blues player back at that time, and his name was ringing all through the Delta: "Charley Patton! Charley Patton!" He played for all the country dances.

He made chords that didn't too many people make, and made lot of chords that he made up hisself, and he made 'em, and it worked. . . . Yeah, you get in the books, you can find some of 'em; some of 'em that you couldn't find, you know what I mean? It's like a lot of musicians, they're good musicians, they can't read—they play, they make chords, they don't know what they're making, but it works.

He dressed clean, wore his hair out, curled to the side. He was Indian. He had some good-looking women—I used to go with one of his women, lived in Merigold, Mississippi.

HOMESICK JAMES: The first time I met Charley was with Johnny Temple. Johnny take me to see Charley Patton at a picnic. They was having a picnic, and I seen all the dust jumping and flying, and it was Charley Patton, he was making all that noise. Charley was something, yes he was.

At that time there wasn't no fancy dressing, but whatever he had, it was clean, you know? But when he got through it would be dirty, 'cause he'd get to wallowing on the ground when he played: he's throwing the guitar so it gets all up behind his back, and get down sometimes—when I seen all this dust going up, the guitar's laying on the ground and he was up on top of it, jumping, playing—that's what he was doing, kicking that dust up with his feet! Charley was a good showman.

KENNY CANNON: My aunt Bessie would say that Charley Patton was the ultimate showman. He could play the guitar—I'll say it like she said it—he could *pick* the guitar with his mouth, with his hands, behind his back, crawling, laying on the floor, simulating different acts. . . . That he was like a one-man band, right? That when you hear his music, you would hear more than just a guitar, you would hear drums, you would hear different licks. That he was so talented that everyone in the area would bid for his show. The stories I hear were, like, he would be scheduled to perform on the weekend for all the sharecroppers, and his music was so loved by everyone in this area that the white plantation owners, they would have weddings or birthday parties and they wanted entertainment and they would, like, almost go into bidding wars for Charley to come and perform at their celebrations.

HOMESICK JAMES: Oh, man! People used to come from miles away. You know peoples talk, and the news get around, where was he gonna be playing at: "This guy's gonna be at—" Hear that name and just stampede. They would come in wagons, horseback. . . . Man, if you would get to the places, you'd see so many mules hooked outside t' the post, the rail, wagons, loads of people. That's the way you got around. There wasn't no car—couldn't come in no car 'cause you didn't have any.

He was a really tough guy, Charley Patton. I didn't see it, but they told me—he was a mule skinner. He worked on the farm, and somebody said that that guy knocked a mule down one time. I heard that, I didn't see that, but he's rowdy enough to do it.

I'LL SHOW YOU COMMON WOMEN HOW I FEEL,

GOING TO GET ME ANOTHER WOMAN BEFORE I LEAVE . . .

I'M GONNA MOVE TO ALABAMA,

I'M GONNA MOVE TO ALABAMA,

I'M GONNA MOVE TO ALABAMA,

MAKE GEORGIA BE YOUR HOME.

—CHARLEY PATTON, "GOING TO MOVE TO ALABAMA," 1929

HONEYBOY EDWARDS: Well, Charley, he drank a lot of whiskey, a lot of white whiskey. And he'd break up his own dances—he'd fight. He'd get to playing the guitar and somebody say, "You wanna fight?" He'd break up his own dances. That's how—1934, I was nineteen years old—he had got to fighting at Holly Ridge and some guy had cut him here on the throat.

He recorded that same winter in Jackson for H. C. Speir—Bertha Lee, his wife, recorded with him, she made the "Yellow Bee Blues," behind Memphis Minnie—and he come back, and Charley died in 1934, in March.* He was living with his uncle, Sherman Patton, at Holly Ridge. And I went through there a week after he died and saw the grave there where they buried him at.

BERNARD: It was striking to me that even within his own community Patton seemed to be recalled as a larger-than-life character. Researchers have established that, although he did get his throat cut, that happened several years before his death, but it has become this legend, and on the whole I had a sense that musicians in this world had a really special stature.

There was a striking contrast between our experience with the older members of the Cannon family, who were very hesitant to talk with us about the old days, and the way the musicians talked. We tend to think of blues musicians as representatives of that black, rural Delta

---

* Most sources list Patton's death date as April 28, 1934.

world, but most of the people in that world were stuck out on the plantations, leading this very limited existence, and the musicians were constantly traveling—Homesick James talked about seeing Blind Lemon Jefferson in Texas, and Honeyboy had stories of hoboing all over the South and Midwest.

The musicians were also very accustomed to dealing with white people. When I asked Robert Lockwood if they ever played for white customers in the old days, he laughed and said, "That's what we was hired by most times. You didn't know that? Shit, my clientele's been white damn near all my life!" He even told a story about playing for the police—and again, it's striking the way he wove this sort of legendary tale. Because Robert Lockwood was a very important figure in Delta blues—he was a protégé of Robert Johnson, who was his stepfather, and had a radio show called *King Biscuit Time* with the harmonica player Sonny Boy Williamson that was the most important showcase for African American music in that whole region for many years—and the way he told the story was a sort of performance in itself.

ROBERT LOCKWOOD: The first fish fry we played, me and Sonny Boy got together—before we started recording, before we got on KFFA—we was in Mississippi, 51 highway, and they put us in jail. They put us in jail to keep some music there, because they had nothing but jukeboxes. And the first weekend we was in jail, we went upstairs and opened the windows and start to playing. Then the people heard and the people ganged around the jail, and we come downstairs and they's throwing money over the fence. When the cops seen that, they decided to take us serenading. They'd take us out serenading every night, and bring us back to the jail, and we'd get out and go in. And we had girlfriends coming in the jail and all that stuff.

So when we left from down there, we had close to a thousand dollars apiece. They put us in jail for vagrancy, but that was only to keep the music there for a while. So when they finally decided to let us go, we got up to the state line of Tennessee—we was hitchhiking—and they come up there and got us, carried us back down there. We played a fish fry and then they brought us back up there and put us out.

BERNARD: There was something surreal about sitting with those three legendary Delta bluesmen in a charming country inn in the Lake District, hearing stories of a time and place more than seventy years and almost five thousand miles away, and trying to imagine the changes they had seen in the course of their lives. The songs they heard Charley Patton play at fish fries were picked up by local players like Son House, Robert Johnson, Lockwood, Howlin' Wolf, and Pops Staples, spread throughout the United States, and became the foundation of blues, rock, gospel, and soul. These men who grew up sharecropping and working with mules now flew around the world, hailed as master musicians by audiences unimaginably different from their neighbors in Mississippi, and were used to being treated as peers and forefathers by international pop stars.

I was also struck, both in this interview and in the conversations with Kenny and Tracy Cannon, by the different ways this music is regarded by white and black audiences. So often, when you go to an African American concert and it's an artist who's been around for many years, the audience is almost entirely white—the black audience has left. And so many of the players who are keeping the Delta blues style alive today are white. I was interested to hear what the older musicians thought about that.

HONEYBOY EDWARDS: Some of the white boys getting a lot of hits from the black music, but I don't know . . . A lot of the boys that are playing the blues now—the blues is not made to be played fast. The blues is supposed to be made to be played slow. And people get running with the blues so fast, they set the chords down so fast that it ain't got a sound. Because it ain't got the time to cook—just get up and get down, get up and get down, and they be jerking and going on, you know, and hitting on nothing. You know what I mean? If you got music that cooks, when you make a chord, you got to let that chord set there and have a feeling from it. Now, they're fast on fingers, but it's not there long enough to sound good.

HOMESICK JAMES: The notes are stacked on top of each other. Blablablablablablah. Too quick.

HONEYBOY EDWARDS: And very few of 'em can sing. Very few of 'em got a voice like us, just a few. . . . I'm not a doctor, but what I *think*, their voice cords are not like ours. Know what I mean? That's the reason they can't control it. They can play but they can't—you'll catch some white boy can sing good, but just a few of 'em now.

HOMESICK JAMES: Didn't holler behind the mules. They don't plow the mules. And that's what makes the voice. See? They ain't done hollered behind a mule, "Hey! Whoa! Haw! Gee! Get over there!"

TRACY CANNON: Blues, for a lot of African Americans, represented freedom and an ability to express themselves, and a release from the drudgery of working in cotton fields in the Deep South—but the African American culture is a very forward-looking culture. I'm wondering if it's not rooted in the pain of our history: there's always been this pain associated with different eras in the African American experience. Like, I don't think the fifties were the rocking-rolling fifties for African Americans—we couldn't drink out of water fountains, you know? The same water fountains as Caucasian people did. So the perspective is different, and I think that's why I just was never really interested in the blues until I met my husband.

Once we started researching Charley Patton, we now regularly listen to blues. There's a respect you've got to have for where you came from, and maybe that's why we, as a culture, haven't fully arrived, because we don't give credence to where we came from as much as we should. But I think it's a double-edged sword, because we've always been able to find a good time in a bad time: while the situation outside of us was really bad, we had to manage to find ways to make it palatable and to make it bearable to us, and one of the big ways was through the music. But I still think that we enjoy that music for the time, and then when there is another time, we take it for what it was and move on.

The translation from blues all the way to rock and now to hip-hop was just a metamorphosis and a culmination of the entire African American experience that was rooted in slavery, and I think the genres are very similar. Blues musicians sang about the hard life on a plantation, and their women, and their drinks, and their fun, and rappers today basically rap about the same things. It's just a different format than it was a hundred years ago: the vernacular has changed, but the message is still the same. I think that we've always found a way to scream through the music, and that screaming has permeated the entire American culture.

Bernard MacMahon interviews Homesick, Lockwood, and Honeyboy

CHANT OF THE SNAKE DANCE:
THE HOPI INDIAN CHANTERS

Hopi Land

LEIGH KUWANWISIWMA: As a Hopi person, you grow up into music. You are born into music, and tradition has the parents, the grandparents, and extended family always singing to the infant. They say that the mother will begin singing to her baby when it's still in the womb. . . . I remember hearing my parents sing cradlesongs, and then as you grew up, then other types of song.

We say that people are brought into this earth with song, and then we do messages to the natural environment, to the trees, the plants, insects, animals, birds, the cosmos, the clouds with song. That's the way we talk to them. . . . I grew up into hard work, and we're taught that when we plant the seeds, we plant them into the womb of earth, and when they sprout and start growing, they're our children. So it's a human relationship with the plants. I was taught that when you're out in the field, always think about songs. Hum to yourself or actually sing a song.

E. J. SATALA: It goes like, when you throw a rock into the water and then there's ripples go out—that's how that song will go out to everybody, and they'll be blessed.

BERNARD: Since childhood I have loved Native American culture, which I was introduced to, wholly inaccurately, by Hollywood Westerns. I loved the sound of drums and the chants, and empathized with the Native American story and what happened to them. So when this project started to take shape, I wanted to look at a Native American recording from the 1920s, but I found that there weren't that many actually recorded commercially. There were plenty of field recordings by anthropologists, but very little was issued by the record companies. One of the few I could find was by a group from Oklahoma, Big Chief Henry's Indian String Band, who recorded a unique hybrid piece called "Indian Tom Tom," with traditional chanting backed by

Big Chief Henry's Indian String Band

fiddles and guitars. It's a wonderful record, and they also did a banjo piece called "Cherokee Rag" that was a favorite of Charlie Poole, one of the great early hillbilly banjo players and bandleaders.

So that was interesting, but then I was visiting Michael Kieffer in Los Angeles and he played me a record by a group simply billed as "Hopi Indian Chanters," with "Chant of the Eagle Dance" on one side and "Chant of the Snake Dance" on the other. It was just chanting and percussion, and I was mesmerized. I got my own copy and played it over and over, and as the *American Epic* project took shape, I thought, "That's a detective challenge. I wonder if we could actually find some people who played on this record, when all you have to go on is 'Hopi Indian Chanters.'"

There was one further clue: in parentheses, the performers were listed as "Group of M. W. Billingsley." At that time there was no mention of M. W. Billingsley on the web, but it was all I had to go on, so I kept searching, and a few months later an estate sale came up with some letters, photographs, and Billingsley's self-published book, *Behind the Scenes in Hopi Land*. That turned out to be an interesting story in itself: Milo Billingsley had grown up on a farm in Iowa, and ran away from home when he was fourteen to join the Hopi. He got himself to Winslow, Arizona, walked into a trading post, and persuaded a Hopi boy to take him to a nearby village, and he lived there for six weeks before his irate father tracked him down and brought him home. When he turned eighteen he went back, learned the language, was adopted into the Hopi nation, and became an advocate for the traditional culture.

It reminded me of the story of Art Satherley, one of the great record scouts for Paramount and Columbia, who saw Buffalo Bill's Wild West Show when it came to Britain in the very early twentieth century and was so enchanted by the Native Americans that he later said that was what inspired him to want to go to America.

Billingsley's book didn't mention any recordings, but he did write about taking a group of Hopis to Washington, D.C., in 1926, because Congress was trying to ban the snake dance and he wanted to prevent that. It was the best clue I had, so I called a trading post on the Hopi reservation to see if they could steer me to someone who would know more—but as soon as I mentioned Billingsley's name they just stopped talking to me. I tried contacting other people but kept getting the same reaction: when I mentioned Billingsley they were kind of polite but said that they'd get back to me, and I never heard from them again.

Hubbell trading post, Winslow, Arizona

M. W. Billingsley

Finally, we heard that a group of Hopi elders was holding a meeting in Flagstaff to discuss the preservation of their language, and decided just to go there. We were pretty much the only white people in the room, and it was a fascinating discussion about the problem of young people not being fluent in Hopi and what they could do to keep the culture from being eroded.

During the breaks I met a couple of elders and they were sort of guardedly friendly, but when I brought up the Billingsley record, they were very negative about it. One very impressive white-haired man said, "This was a very bad day in our history, that these sacred songs were recorded. We are not happy about what happened there." But eventually I met one man, an elder named E. J. Satala, who was very welcoming and warm, and I invited him out to dinner and played him the recordings, and showed him the little bits and pieces I'd collected on Billingsley, and he was really interested—though he told me that the song billed as the snake dance on the record label was actually the eagle dance, and the song billed as the eagle dance was the buffalo dance.

I told him about the difficulties I'd been having, and he explained that the Hopi do not like to share their history and their world with outside people, and that even within the culture much of their knowledge is guarded very closely.

LEIGH KUWANWISIWMA: We are a very private society, and that's the way it should be. We have different societies, and they all have their own way, and a lot of it is secluded: I know very little about some of these esoteric societies, and that's okay, because that knowledge is only for those priesthoodships, and with that knowledge that they embody, they take care of everybody. . . . That's what keeps it strong. If we just pour it out, then it's tainted, and we can't allow that to happen.

E. J. SATALA: When you get initiated you can't talk about that ceremony to another person that's not initiated. In my case, I can't talk to people from another village, even—they may be initiated in their village, but they haven't gone through the ceremony that I went through. . . . You keep those to yourself, and that way that religion or that ceremony stays sacred.

BERNARD: It was becoming clear that this would be a difficult story to explore on film, but I asked E. J. Satala if we could come to the reservation and do an interview on camera, and he said he would consider it. There are very strict rules about even taking photographs on the reservation, so I realized it might not work out, but we began making plans to bring a crew to Hopi.

Meanwhile, I heard that an anthropological get-together in Arizona had included the screening of a color film from the early 1950s of Billingsley presenting some Hopi dancers,

SEE OTHER SIDE

34068-N

hosted by an archaeologist named Ken Zoll. I got in touch with him, and it turned out that he had tracked down a niece of Billingsley's and had this giant scrapbook filled with photographs and newspaper clippings, including articles about the performance for Congress and photographs of Billingsley with the five dancers who had appeared there. That performance had happened only a few weeks after the Hopi Indian Chanters recorded in New York, and it had to be on the same tour, so I now had photographs of the men who had made that record, and some of the newspaper articles also included their names—though generally in pretty garbled forms.

The photographs of the Washington performance included a panoramic shot of the audience, and it was clearly a major event with thousands of people watching, so I began wondering if someone might have filmed it. That was another quest, but eventually I found an archive that had the raw rushes for a newsreel—as far as I can tell it had never been edited and shown, but there was about four minutes of footage, and it was amazing: you see this huge audience, just like the photograph, and then you see Billingsley come out in this kind of Hollywood Western regalia to make the presentation, and then the Hopi come out and begin to do their dances. It's an odd mix—for one dance they are wearing feathered war bonnets, which are not part of the Hopi tradition—and I'm watching this, and then they open a box and bring out some snakes, and you see the snakes crawling on the stage, and I'm like, "Oh my God, they're doing the snake dance!" That was startling, because all the dances are sacred, but the snake dance is the most sacred.

By now we had the record, the film, and all these photographs and news articles, and we were ready to go to Hopi.

ALLISON: I've traveled all over the world, but the drive out to Hopi felt like the most foreign place I've ever been, almost like landing on the moon. It is high desert, very arid and empty, and it is beautiful in its way, but also feels very forbidding. There is this long, very straight road, and it just seems to go on forever, and there is no sign of any habitation, and these huge, strange rock formations. Then you see the mesas rising out of the desert—these vast, flat plateaus with very steep sides—and there was this furious wind blowing, and all this dust whirling around. And you can't imagine how anyone could possibly live there.

E. J. SATALA: When I was in high school and we started going on field trips to different places, and we saw, like, in New Mexico—it was in an area that had trees, and you knew that there would be animals in there, deer and elk and bear, and there was water flowing, and we thought about that. And [we] came home and asked one of the elders, and the elder shared with us that Hopi life is meant to be hard. . . . That's why it's way out here, where there's no rain,

and you have to pray, and really believe in what you're doing—that belief has to be there, and that's what makes the rain come and the plants grow.

ALLISON: We had arranged an appointment at the Hopi Cultural Center, and the first person we met there actually wasn't Hopi. He was there to screen visitors, and he explained that basically his job was to say no—to explain to people why they couldn't take photos or films, or record anything. But then we got an interview with the director of the Cultural Preservation Office, Leigh Kuwanwisiwma, and he was a bit distant at first, but when we told him about the film and what we were trying to do, he became quite interested. He knew about Billingsley and the trip to Washington and the whole story.

LEIGH KUWANWISIWMA: What [originally] triggered the interest into Hopi was President Teddy Roosevelt visiting the Hopi villages and witnessing a snake dance. Of course, during his visit he had press coverage; it publicized the Hopi culture pretty much in a way that cultures were always portrayed as "exotic," and it triggered off a huge tourist stream into Hopi. The Santa Fe Railroad promoted the snake dance, and they were doing postcards with footage or pictures of the snake dance. . . .

M.W. Billingsley and his group of Hopi Snake Danc[e]
Arizona Cliff Dweller's Village
N.Y. World's Fair '39.

It was part of this whole period of what history calls "manifest destiny": the movement towards the West was about land, it was about material wealth, and the tribes just simply were in the way. So it ended up with warfare against the plains—when you read back into that history, it was terrible. . . .

The government began to size up that you ain't going to break the Hopis unless you break their culture. So this is where they began to take a look at some of the ceremonies, because they realized that the villages were consolidated: they had the kivas, they had religion there, they had the kinship system. So they began to target some of these major ritual ceremonies, to ban them.

Of course, early on, everybody was called a "savage"—our intellect was supposed to be lower than other people, and that played into this whole game from Washington. The snake ceremony was one of the first to be targeted. They labeled this a "cult"—all of our ceremonies are about rain, about corn, about life, a good life for everybody, but of course they didn't understand anything about these ceremonies. . . .

Billingsley was around and he was the one that learned about the political issues and the march towards banning these ritual ceremonies. He was sharing that information with the snake priests, and they were really scared, they were intimidated. . . . This was their duty, to perform these dances, so it was a real threat. That's what convinced our leaders to actually go to Washington, to demonstrate that their dance, the snake dance, was not about evil, it wasn't occult. They wanted to tell Washington that these dances are also for you.

HOPI INDIANS DANCE ON CAPITOL PLAZA

EXOTIC PERFORMANCE IS STAGED BEFORE WASHINGTON CROWD TO PROVE THEIR RITES NOT CRUEL

New York Times: *May 15 [1926]—The Capitol plaza was transformed today into a bit of the Far West by five Hopi Indians from the cliffs and pueblos of Arizona. Before a crowd that included Vice President Dawes . . . Justices Sanford, Holmes and Sutherland of the United States Supreme Court, Senators and Congressmen innumerable, and some 5,000 other citizens. . . .*

All of the panoply and paraphernalia of the red men were there—the bows and arrows, the moccasins, the feathered, variegated war bonnets, the gaudy head bands, bear skins which formed smocks, small bells strung around the bodies, the war whoops, and six Arizona black snakes that were caressed by the dance leader and then coiled and squirmed across the small platform as the Indians wove back and forth and swayed to the beat of a tom-tom. . . .

The purpose of the exhibition, Senator Cameron of Arizona explained, was to show that the rites and ceremonies of the Hopis are not inhuman or cruel, as has been contended by organizations which seek to have the Government prevent the annual performance. He said the dance was not as bad as the Charleston. . . .

BERNARD: From the newspaper articles, Leigh was able to identify four of the five dancers, and he said they still had descendants living on the reservation, but they might not want to talk with us. He also suggested that as a way of placating the government the dancers might have substituted a less sensitive ceremony or created some kind of hybrid for the event, rather than performing the authentic snake dance. But when we showed him the film he was obviously moved. The first thing that struck him was the watching crowd.

Hopi Indians to Be Here On Way to Washington. Show at Maryland Tuesday

The uncanny dances of this people are a part of a religious ritual, but purists are alleging that they are immoral.

Ancient signal fires are burning and long-silent drums are booming on the Hopi Indian reservation, in northern Arizona.

For the first time in generations, the Red Man has refused to obey the "Great White Father" in Washington.

The Department of the Interior and the Commission of Indian Affairs have issued orders demanding that the Hopi give up their old religion with its weird religious dances.

Through a council of their chiefs and tribal governors, the Indians have answered, and the substance of their answer is:

"You can punish us, you can put us in jail, you can kill us, you can wipe us out and destroy us—but as long as we live you can never make us do this thing!

"If you persist in your order we declare war. We are too weak for physical battle. We know that our arrows and tomahawks are futile against your machine guns and cannons But we will go to war with you in the courts and fight you to the end.

"We prefer the Happy Hunting Grounds to the Heaven of our white brothers. The golden streets of your Heaven would soon wear out moccasins, and the jeweled walls of your New Jerusalem would be only a prison for our souls."

The formal refusal of the Hopi, couched in more legal language, has been received in Washington and has created a big problem.

It is complicated by the fact that powerful individuals and influences have rushed to the defense of the Indians

Influential society women, led by Mrs. Willard D. Straight, one of the Whitneys; Irving Bacheller and Mrs. Mary Austin, novelists; artists, including George Bellows, Remington Schuyler, Catherine Critcher and others; Mrs. Walston Brown, Mrs. James Lees Laidlaw and Mrs. Henry Phipps; distinguished ethnologists, both of the Smithsonian Institute and the American Museum of Natural History, have all come into the fight to preserve the ancient traditions and tribal dances of the Indians.

LEIGH KUWANWISIWMA: You have men in ties, suit coats, cigars, nice hats. The ladies are dressed for a very, very big occasion. As I look at the film I kind of smile, because it appears, even back then, the government's controlled by wealthy people. . . .

The first one of the Hopi Indian chanters looks to be Kotsheptewa—that means "the gray rolling thunderclouds ready to give us rain." He was the head snake priest, the society leader from the village of Mishongnovi and was a very good friend of Billingsley. Then you have Salaptotsi, which literally means "spruce shoes," but probably in context it means "someone who has the pathway to the spruce people." Then Si'tala is the vision of the horizon full of all kinds of flowers; it means "beauty, a vision of a good way of life." And then Pongya literally means "an altar," but I'm sure it means a story about a certain type of altar; it's probably a ritual name. . . .

Now we have the buffalo [dancers]. These are the buffaloes from the village of Mishongnovi, where Kotsheptewa was from. . . . This one is the Comanche dance. . . .

Medicine man

Sohu "buffalo dancer"

Chief Kolchaftewa

Chief chanter

Snake priest

Now, this is the representation of the snake dance. The first ones are the antelope priests, and then the second group, the three are snake priests. . . . They're getting the snakes. This is the actual performances of the ceremony. . . .

It's sad to see. I've read the paper records of this, because we have a file on Billingsley, but to see the actual footage is just pretty overwhelming. . . . That Hopis had to go up to that level of actually presenting a highly esoteric dance to tell others that this is the Hopi way. The history talks about it, and now on-screen it's the reality of what the Hopis had to do. They had no choice . . . the threat to the Hopi people, and pretty much being forced to "prove their way of life" through an actual public performance for others. . . . No one should ever be forced to do that—never, nobody.

BERNARD: It was a very emotional experience, watching that film with Leigh and seeing him actually moved to tears. But even more moving, for me, was what happened next, which was that he told us we should use that film in our documentary. We gave him a copy, and said we would never show it without his permission, but he said, "I think people need to see what our people had to go through." It was an incredibly powerful gesture.

That was really the end of this story for us. We could have continued with the original plan to find relatives of the Hopi who made that journey with Billingsley, and I'm sure we could have found some people, but I very much doubt that they would have felt comfortable talking with us about it. Even E. J. Satala was very circumspect in his conversations with us. Leigh seemed to be regarded as the one person who was supposed to discuss these sorts of things with outsiders.

As for Billingsley, we came away with the sense that he was quite an ambivalent figure. Our first impression was that people remembered him very negatively, but when Leigh talked about him, it was as someone who was a friend to the Hopi and had done them a service by acting as a go-between with the government and helping them to demonstrate that their ceremonies were not barbaric or savage. Then, watching him on film, it was clear that Billingsley enjoyed the limelight and the prestige of setting up these big meetings with Congress and being recognized as an authority and a representative of Hopi.

The film from 1926 was silent, but when he was filmed again thirty years later, introducing a group of dancers that still included his friend Kotsheptewa, he was wearing the same flashy regalia, and his presentation has a whiff of P. T. Barnum.

M. W. BILLINGSLEY: Now we present the sacred snake ceremony as held within the kivas or temples of the Hopi—something that no white person or Indian has ever witnessed before unless they be a member of the secret snake clan. . . . The placing of the live snakes in their

Hopi delegation at the Capitol (from left to right): *Billingsley, Edythe Sterling, Kotsheptewa, Arizona senator Ralph Cameron, Salaptotsi, Vice President Charles Dawes, House Speaker Nicholas Longworth, Si'tala, Qömakwaptiwa, and Pongya*

mouths is to convey to the snake the thought of brotherly love or friendship; it is not snake worship. This is your first opportunity as well as your last to witness this ancient rite. . . .

BERNARD: I never really sorted out the contradictions between this idea that the snake dance is a very private ceremony that should never be seen by outsiders and the fact that it was performed for Roosevelt in 1913 and became a huge tourist attraction. Leigh told us that up through the 1980s there would be tour buses lined up for a mile, and for a while he actually stopped attending the ceremonies because there were so many tourists that there was no room for Hopis.

Perhaps the answer is that the ceremony can exist on different levels and have different meanings—or perhaps the answer is something we do not need to understand. That phonograph record that first sent us on this journey continues to move me, and Leigh clearly regarded it as an important historical document. But he also linked both the film and the recording to

the larger project of "manifest destiny," as part of an effort to salvage and preserve Hopi lore that simultaneously relegates it to a disappearing past. As director of the Cultural Preservation Office, much of his work is repatriating and archiving these materials, but he emphasized that his more important duty was to keep the underlying traditions alive.

LEIGH KUWANWISIWMA: We have this recording from 1926, and this song is regularly played on our Hopi radio, and today we still carry on the buffalo dance and this style of singing. It makes me feel good that this song goes back in time, and we're still at it, we're still creating buffalo songs.

Hopi snake priests perform a Plains Indian dance in front of the Capitol with the leader Kotsheptewa playing a drum

A lot of the interest in the Hopi is because the whole world—in particular the American culture—has created a huge religious vacuum, [and] they just yearn for some kind of way to deal with the chaos of today. The dominant cultures live day to day, but the Hopi people remember the past; we're thankful for today, and we're also looking at the future. That's what the Hopi culture is about.

That's, I guess, the motivation for a few of us to continue to talk publicly. Our teachings as Hopi people say that the Hopis will be the last of the indigenous cultures, and because of that we're told to keep our traditions, keep our culture, keep our language alive, because we'll be the final way of life in North and South America, and perhaps all over the world.

8 BIRD OF PARADISE: JOSEPH KEKUKU

Joseph Kekuku

BERNARD: I fell in love with the sound of the steel guitar on a Flying Burrito Brothers album, *The Gilded Palace of Sin*. It was one of the most beautiful sounds I'd ever heard, and I wanted to hear more of that, and that took me to Hawaiian music. I started listening to records of early Hawaiian artists: first Sol K. Bright, who led a popular group in Hollywood in the 1930s, and the steel guitar virtuoso Sol Hoʻopiʻi, and then Kalama's Quartet, for the vocal harmonizing. That also connected with other music I'd loved as a child, the soundtrack to *South Pacific*—which of course is not Hawaiian, but conjured up this incredibly romantic picture of the Pacific islands.

I was intrigued by the origin of that steel guitar style, and how it had developed and spread into all these other kinds of music. It is such a distinctive sound, but has become associated with everything from country and western to Delta blues, all the way to Pink Floyd's "Wish You Were Here." And when I began looking into it, I found most authorities agreeing that it was invented by a specific person, Joseph Kekuku, when he was just a young boy. I wanted to know more about him, and I found a few articles and mentions in various books, and then Michael Kieffer in Los Angeles, who had first turned me on to many of the early Hawaiian recordings, introduced me to Kekuku's great-great-cousin, Alyssa Beth Archambault.

ALYSSA BETH ARCHAMBAULT: I grew up learning about my great-grandparents, Sam Nainoa and Eugenia Nainoa. They were born in Laʻie, Oʻahu, and Sam Nainoa had a first cousin by the name of Joseph Kekuku, who was three years older than he was, born in 1874. Both Joseph and Sam were very musical as children, and they started playing the standard Hawaiian guitar, what is called "slack key" [because the players loosen some strings to create open chords and unique tunings], not yet the steel. Sam also played the violin, and as kids they grew up playing together as musical partners and good friends.

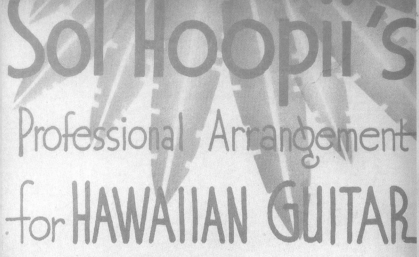

Sol Hoopii's
Professional Arrangement for HAWAIIAN GUITAR

Sol K. Bright

1929   Sol Bri

Sol Ho'opi'i (above)

Sam Nainoa (seated, center) *with the Kamehameha School band* (right)

OLIVER·MOROSCO'S·PRODUCTION
THE BIRD
OF
PARADISE
BY
RICHARD·WALTON·TULLY

LL (Aloha Oe) 60
G LOVE (Ali Wela) 50
ME NOT (Mai Polia Oe) .70
AN HULA (Instrumental) .60

293354

6

HIGH-CLASS
HAWAIIAN CONCERT
Galt Theatre

To= night ONLY

Friday Oct. 27

"KAMUELA" NAINOA

A native Hawaiian from our island possesions, the Hawaiian Islands, with his steel guitar and featurinig the NATIVE DANCE of his people. Direct from seven-weeks engagement at GRAUMAN MILLION DOLLAR THE-ATRE of Los Angeles.

SOME OF THE SELECTIONS

Hawaiian Folk Songs (not in Print), Brach Waikiki, The Sheik, The Blues, Three o'Clock in the Morning, Leave Me With a Kick, I Wish I Knew, Kiss Me Again, The Stars and Stripes Forever, March of Hawaii, with drums and bugle imitations, By The Sapphire Sea, Aloa Oe (Farewell to Thee), Ragtime Playing, with one hand, and many others. Rosary, Mockingbird.

Also Feature Pictures

Admission: Adults 27c, Tax 3c, Total 30c
Child'n 13c, Tax 2c, Total 15c

The story is that when Joseph was eleven years old he happened to be walking down a railroad track and he had his guitar and he picked up, for some reason, a metal bolt on the tracks, and at some point the bolt hit the strings of the guitar and it made a sound that caught his ear. So he took it home and started to play with that bolt on the neck of the guitar and just explore the sounds that came out of it.

He experimented with all sorts of objects: a metal comb, a pocketknife, and the neighboring kids were starting to hear what he was doing and were also curious, and they started to try to create those same sounds. So it created sort of a friendly competition between everyone in the village, and it actually inspired Joseph to master the technique of the steel guitar. It took him seven years, using several different metal objects, and he also changed out the strings—they were nylon originally and he changed them out to be steel, and he also lifted the nut [that the strings pass over at the top of the guitar neck] so that the strings weren't so close to the neck, and he turned the guitar horizontal and put it on his lap, facing up.

SIMEON NAWAʻA, recalling Joseph Kekuku in 1944: I entered the Kamehameha School for Boys in the fall of 1888. The following fall . . . two lads from Laʻie, on the windward side of Oʻahu, came to our school—Joseph Kekuku, the guitar player, and Samuel Nainoa, the violinist. They were good entertainers, and to our astonishment Joe, besides playing the guitar the ordinary way, would shift to running a hair comb or tumbler on the strings producing a sweet sound, while Sam, the accompanist, followed him with his violin.*

ALYSSA BETH ARCHAMBAULT: Joseph eventually came to develop the steel bar, which he made [in the metal shop] at Kamehameha School, and he played for local school performances and for his family, and he taught Sam Nainoa how to play the steel guitar.

As they got older, it really caught fire to all the foreigners that were coming to the islands, and they were invited to go to the mainland and share their music, the Hawaiian music. So in 1904, Joseph went to the mainland and performed in all sorts of renowned theaters across the country—in L.A., in Chicago, in New York—and eventually he started doing a show called *The Bird of Paradise*, and it was such a huge hit that he was invited to London, where he played in front of the kings and queens.

While he was doing that, Sam Nainoa was here performing in all the theaters on the islands with his wife, my great-grandmother Eugenia—he was a musician and a composer and an orchestra director, and she was his hula dancer. And while he was playing in Honolulu, a

---

* Letter to the *Honolulu Star-Bulletin*, October 21, 1944, reprinted in Lorene Ruymar, ed., *The Hawaiian Steel Guitar and Its Great Hawaiian Musicians*. (Anaheim, CA: Centerstream, 1996), 5.

From left to right: *Unknown ukulele player, Hannah "Toots" Paka, Joseph Kekuku* (seated), *and July Paka*

showman from New York invited him to come to the mainland, too. So in 1911 to 1912, my great-grandfather and his wife packed up and went to the mainland. It was supposed to be two months on the road, across the country, so they left their nine children with Sam's father, Lyons Baldwin Nainoa, to raise them until they returned. But that two months never came, and Sam and Eugenia lived out the rest of their life on the mainland.

They toured the country, from West Coast to East Coast, and had four more children on the road. Only two of them survived, and my grandmother was the youngest, Ula Jewel Nainoa, and she actually became my great-grandfather's prodigy in the steel guitar, and her sister, Joyce, played the ukulele and the bass. So they were all touring as a family around the country, and then eventually settled in Los Angeles.

When my great-grandfather left the islands, he never came back, and he left nine kids behind, so it really left a hole in his heart. We'll never know why he didn't come back—maybe he was too poor—but, you know, it created a distance between the family in Hawai'i and the new family he started on the mainland. And I'm a part of the family on the mainland. I grew up with my great-grandfather's steel guitars on the wall and a big poster of my great-grandmother, her

THE BIRD OF PARADISE

The Bird of Paradise *review, London*

LUANA ABOUT TO SACRIFICE
HERSELF INTO THE VOLCANO'S MOU

LF FOR HER PEOPLE BY THROWING

S AN OFFERING TO THE GODDESS PELE.

vaudeville posters, and their recordings, and all my relatives "talking story" around us, so that was ingrained in me early on.

Growing up knowing that there was a distance between the family, it was hard knowing we were separated for so long. And about fifteen years ago I decided to come over to the islands and meet my family for the first time, and tell them about their family on the mainland, and to learn about my family here.

ALLISON: We flew to Hawai'i right after our visit to Hopi, and you couldn't imagine two more different places on the planet—one dry and desolate, with no rain, and then you arrive in Hawai'i and it's just a paradise. We arrived totally exhausted, because we'd had this long drive from Hopi to Phoenix, where we had to back up all our interviews and get all our gear to FedEx and shipped over to Hawai'i, along with ourselves and our crew. So we arrived rather tired and bedraggled, and we were driving up to La'ie, along the east coast of the island, and that's a stunning drive: you have steep, fluted, green-covered mountains on one side, and gentle turquoise lapping ocean on the other, with white-sand beaches, and a couple of times our crew just stopped and jumped in the water. We couldn't believe it, after traveling across America, cramped together in a van, to have arrived somewhere that beautiful. It was almost like a parody of itself—you have the glorious foliage and exotic flowers of the rain forest, and the warm Pacific Ocean, and when we were filming the interview with Alyssa, a rainbow came out above her.

It was another instance of the music seeming to reflect the place: it's got a much slower pace, and it's gentle, like the lapping of the waves—not the big strong waves on the north coast that the surfers go on, but around the other side of the island where Joseph Kekuku was from—and the beautiful flowers and the sounds of the birds.

In La'ie, we met Alyssa's cousin Ka'iwa Meyer, and we saw the house where Joseph had grown up and the store that their family owned. It was quite a small town, and it didn't look like it had changed all that much since the nineteenth century, so you could really get a feeling of what it would have been like at that time.

KA'IWA MEYER: Joseph Kekuku was my grandmother's brother. He was the oldest son and then he had four sisters and another brother. His father was pure Hawaiian—he was the *konohiki* of La'ie, which means he worked for the king and followed all King Kamehameha's rules and regulations. So his father was a very well-known man, he's in books and museums, and his mother was Miriam Kaopua; she was also a pure-blooded Hawaiian, and her line is through King Kamehameha I.

My *tutu*, who is my grandfather, named him Joseph Kekuku because his name was Joseph Kekuku'upenakana'iaupuniokamehameha Apuakehau,* so he gave his son, the oldest one, Joseph Kekuku. . . . So Joseph was born and raised under this type of very close-knitted, structured, family home environment, and they were very respectful and very kind and very loving. They all shared a bowl of poi—one poi, and everybody eats from it with their fingers. . . . He was a man of strong family, so he turned out to be a very strong man also.

Over one hundred years we've had our store in La'ie, and we always sit in front of the store, on the cement, and for breakfast we have soda and *pake* cake. And that's what he did: he was sitting there on the cement floor, playing his old guitar, and his metal comb fell out of his shirt pocket and fell on his guitar and made that noise that he was really intrigued about, and next thing you know, he created the steel guitar.

Can you imagine that? Of all the people in the world, one young kid in La'ie—it's an amazing story. I can't imagine an eleven-year-old going through that, teaching himself. That is powerful. He was a special person, and everyone talks about how kind and caring and loving and gentle and dedicated he was to his music and his steel guitar. And he sacrificed by leaving home to spread it to the U.S. and then to Europe, and now it's all over the world.

Toots Paka Hawaiian Troupe

---

* Most published sources give this full name to the guitarist Joseph Kekuku himself rather than to his father, but research by John Troutman and others suggests that Ka'iwa Meyer's information is more reliable.

Hawaiian guitar school in Omaha, Nebraska, circa 1940

The Electone-Settes

The Kohala Girls

Letritia Kandle and Paul Whiteman

BERNARD: Hawaiian music was incredibly popular in the United States in the early twentieth century; there are some estimates that in the mid-teens Hawaiian records were outselling any other genre. Joseph Kekuku almost certainly appeared on some of those recordings, and it is even likely that he played the steel guitar part on the first surviving Hawaiian sessions, recorded on cylinders by a guitarist named July Paka for the Edison company in 1909. I tracked those down, but unfortunately the steel playing on them is so minimal and hard to hear that it really didn't give me a clear idea of how he sounded.

With Best Wishes

Layton & Johnstone

Turner Layton and Clarence Johnstone

Fortunately, a British newsletter called *Banjo, Guitar, and Mandolin* published a few reminiscences in the 1930s of Kekuku's stay in London, and one of them mentioned that he'd made three records with a duo called Layton and Johnstone, and gave the titles of the songs. Layton and Johnstone were a pair of African American singers who were huge in Britain in my grandmother's time, and their old 78s are all over secondhand stores and on eBay. So I started looking for those three records, and they turned out to be exceptions: they were really hard to find. Eventually I managed to track one of them down, a song called "I'll See You in My Dreams," and on the label it said "American Duettists with Piano and Steel Guitar." It was from 1926, and I had hoped it might be an electrical recording, but it turned out to have been recorded acoustically, but it was really well done and sounded terrific. There's a piano plunking away, and Layton and Johnstone singing in their smooth vaudeville style, and then, halfway through, this steel guitar comes in, clear as a bell. Interestingly, it's not the sort of lyrical, soaring sound we've become used to since—it's quite crude and hard-hitting, and gives you a sense of how those early artists had to play when they wanted to be heard in a large hall or were playing over a full orchestra.

It was an amazing moment, because this was a man who invented a musical instrument that is known all over the world, and in a way this was the first time anyone had really heard him in context. When he made those records, no one could have imagined how important the instrument would become, and afterwards the recordings were forgotten. So I made transfers of the three discs and brought them with us to play for people in Hawai'i. With Alyssa's help we organized an outdoor party, a luau, with Auntie Ka'iwa and some local musicians, and at the height of the luau, I played the records for them.

KA'IWA MEYER: Listening to my uncle play for the first time today was very uplifting and it made me feel teary. . . . I rarely cry anymore, for years and years, because I keep myself in control, but today was an exception to the rule, because I couldn't stop crying. I think that his spirit is with us and that he knows that we're trying to give him recognition for his beautiful music and his steel guitar.

I think it was hard for him and he missed home—he wrote home and everything, told us what he was doing . . . but he stayed there. He was so dedicated to the Hawaiian guitar, and they just loved that sound—they were so in love with Hawai'i and these men who played that steel. You know, it's a way to visualize the beach, the sun, the beautiful paradise, and the people in the mainland, who have snow and cold and tornadoes and all that—it took them away from all that type of natural disaster. . . .

Joseph Kekuku's immigration papers

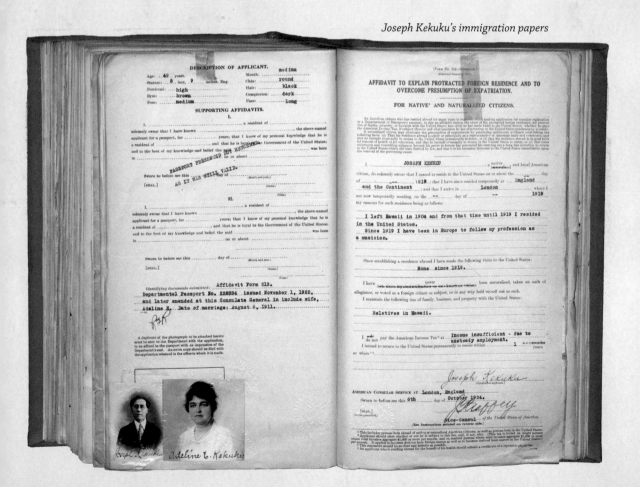

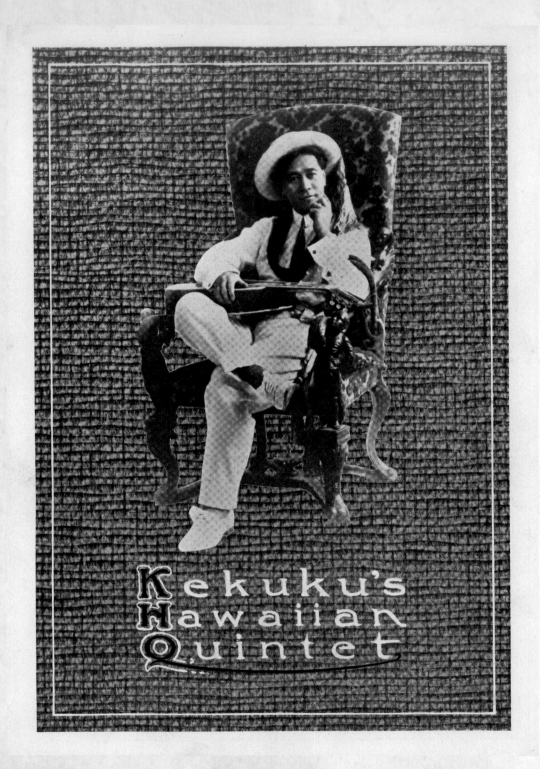

When he came back from Europe, he settled in Dover, New Jersey—I guess maybe because it's on the ocean and it has similar things, like mountains and trees and flowers, on the ocean side. . . . They used to call him Mr. Aloha, and now every year they give him a recognition and honor him as the Hawaiian man who helped their town, and he's very famous in New Jersey. He's buried over there.

So he made a good life for himself in the mainland, [but] it's a different lifestyle; it's very different goals, you know. In Hawai'i we have different priorities: here, it's the family and the land and the culture, and *aloha,** which you don't find on the mainland. Hawai'i is unique, and those who come here that are not of the Hawaiian culture, they feel that warmth. . . . When they come here, it's like, "Wow, these Hawaiians are giving away everything!" It's all about "Come into my house, *e komo mai ka hale*—come into my house and share my food." They leave the keys, the house is open—I remember that as a child growing up. The whole town, we shared everything together.

Back in those days we were one huge, big family—in La'ie there were only Hawaiians that were living there; that was the only culture, and we just loved each other, all of the whole town. That feeling is home, where you share with everyone and everyone's a family. So he gave that aloha to the world: through his music, through his lessons, through his life.

---

* *Aloha* has a broad range of meanings; a partial list in the *Hawaiian Dictionary* published by the University of Hawai'i includes "love," "affection," "compassion," "mercy," "sympathy," "pity," and "kindness"—and it is also used for both "hello" and "good-bye."

9

MAL HOMBRE: LYDIA MENDOZA

BERNARD: For much of this project we were based in Los Angeles, so we were surrounded by Mexican American culture, and I was very much drawn to the range of music that culture has produced. I was particularly struck by the *corridos*, the narrative ballads, which form a sort of musical chronicle of everything that has happened in northern Mexico and the southwestern United States since the late nineteenth century. Chris Strachwitz at Arhoolie Records has released numerous collections of early recordings from Texas and the border region, and they are the most political lyrics I came across from that time—I suspect the American companies that were recording and releasing these things probably didn't know what a lot of the lyrics were about, which was often the American oppression of the Latino people.

One of the most striking artists in the Arhoolie catalog is Lydia Mendoza, a magnificent singer and guitarist who recorded hundreds of songs in a career reaching back to the 1920s, and along with albums of her music over the course of more than half a century, Chris also compiled a book of her reminiscences. I listened to her recordings over and over, and they touched me on a very emotional level. Her voice was so powerful, and she was also an incredible musician. When we were recording the modern sessions, my original idea was

Roger and Ann Hernandez, grandchildren of Lydia Mendoza

to have Ana Gabriel sing one of her songs accompanied by someone playing the twelve-string guitar in Lydia's style, and I had these terrific musicians working with me, but none of them could re-create the feel of her playing.

I asked Chris if he could put me in touch with her family, and he said she had grandchildren living in San Antonio—Roger Hernandez and Ann Hernandez-McKinney. So I called them and arranged a visit. They were living in a Mexican American suburb on the outskirts of San Antonio, in this quaint, modest house, where Lydia had lived for a while toward the end of her life, and it was like a museum to Lydia. It was festooned with pictures and memorabilia, family photographs, and they even had her performance costumes. It was obvious that she had been a huge figure in their lives.

ANN HERNANDEZ-McKINNEY: The greatest memories I have are when we were planning trips on the weekends to go see Grandma in Houston. . . . It'd take us about three hours to get there, and we'd arrive about nine-thirty or ten o'clock to her house, and we'd pull up in the driveway and the only thing you could see was just this one light coming from the bedroom; the whole house would be dark.

We'd jump out of the car and run to the door, and Mom was with us, and she'd knock and

say, "*¿Señora? ¿Señora?*" She'd crack the door and we'd see Grandma with her glasses. She'd be at the sewing table in her room. She'd say, "*¡Ah, ya llegaron! Entre, entran*"—"Come in, come in." And we'd be, "Grandma! Grandma!" She'd have her sewing kit, all her little boxes of sequins—

ROGER HERNANDEZ: They were usually all over the floor—

ANN HERNANDEZ-McKINNEY: She had a mess in her room, but her beautiful dresses were there; she was making them by hand, sewing. And she'd get up. "*Ah, ya vinieron.*" You know, we'd finally arrived. And she'd say, "Come in, everybody come in."

ROGER HERNANDEZ: So then we would call Aunt Nora, 'cause she lived a couple of houses down, and before you knew it someone was making a run to go get donuts, and we would spend the rest of the evening just catching up.

ANN HERNANDEZ-McKINNEY: She made coffee for the grown-ups, she made the Mexican hot chocolate for us, and we were in heaven.

Quarteto Carta Blanca (left to right): *Leonor, Lydia, Francisco, and Maria Mendoza, circa 1919*

ROGER HERNANDEZ: She was a great cook. She did all the bad things that you're not supposed to do now: she would cook the bacon, use the bacon grease to refry the beans, to make the scrambled eggs. She had a tub of that grease in a coffee can on the stove, so you'd just hear it crackling—

ANN HERNANDEZ-McKINNEY: But it smelt good in the house.

ROGER HERNANDEZ: And she made the kind of tortillas that have the flour on them still. She made them by hand, and her tamales—she made pork tamales, she made sweet tamales, she made jalapeño tamales with, like, four jalapeños in each that I couldn't eat. And she didn't measure anything; it was all by feel and touch.

ANN HERNANDEZ-McKINNEY: As kids we didn't speak much Spanish, and when we'd speak to her, she would just look at us. She'd say, *"Háblame en español."* And I'd look at her, and my mom would say, "She wants you to speak to her in Spanish, or she's not gonna answer you." She would just look at us funny. Of course, she knew everything we were saying—she knew English very well—but she just preferred not to speak it. She'd get us—she'd get anyone—and force them to speak back to her in Spanish.

ROGER HERNANDEZ: What I remember is seeing her in her room with a little cassette player, recording her tunes and then playing them back. If she didn't like it, she would fine-tune that little tune or a chord or whatever it was, and then play it back on her little black tape recorder.

ANN HERNANDEZ-McKINNEY: We would go to the bar and grills where she used to sing, and we would be running around, as kids do, having fun, playing chase for a long time, until we got tired. Then it was time for us to relax, and we'd all sit around the stage like little Indians, looking up at her singing, like "There's Grandma, and she's just working and singing." We were used to that, because we listened to her music at home, on the couch or at the kitchen table, just tuning her guitar or just strumming.

ROGER HERNANDEZ: It seems kind of a cliché that we thought everybody's grandmother sang, you know? But it's not till we grew older that I realized the significance of how much of an artist she was and the fans that she had.

Left to right: *Lydia, Juanita, Leonor, Manuel, and Maria Mendoza*

She was born in 1916, in Houston, Texas. She was one of eight children. Her mom, Leonor, played the guitar, and she wanted to play as well, but of course they couldn't afford to buy her a guitar. So she improvised and got a wooden board and nailed nails on each end and got rubber bands and strummed, and pretended. And when she was old enough, her mom finally decided to buy her a guitar. And she taught herself to play.

They were a musically inclined family, and they formed their own *carpa*, a family troupe. They traveled Mexico and southern Texas, particularly the Rio Grande Valley, and they also toured Michigan during the summer months, playing for the migrants that worked up there.

ANN HERNANDEZ-McKINNEY: Back in the day, you know, the migrant workers worked in the cotton fields—

ROGER HERNANDEZ: And vegetable, and fruit—

ANN HERNANDEZ-McKINNEY: They'd be out in the fields, picking the crops, and they had long working days, from the crack of dawn till the sun went down. The conditions were pretty rough out there, and they didn't have much. And Grandma and Great-grandpa and Great-grandma and the brothers and sisters would go out there and perform, to bring some happiness and some joy to them by entertaining them and bringing their beautiful music to them. And the people looked forward to that, because it broke the pattern of all that hard work.

ROGER HERNANDEZ: At that time, Americans just viewed the Mexicans as a subculture and treated them like that. [When they crossed the border] they'd make them wash their hair in gasoline to make sure they didn't have any lice, and Grandma and their family went through that. But they persevered—I mean, that was just part of life and part of having to go back and forth, and making a living. And they did what they had to do.

BERNARD: When I arrived in San Antonio, the first thing that struck me was the variety of buildings. It feels like this fusion of North American and Mexican culture, and the whole city has this commingling of architectural styles. You drive past the Alamo, and there are all these sandy-colored walls, and there are some bigger office buildings, and then you get out into these areas where the houses are painted in vibrant colors. It's got this fantastic kind of frontier feel to it, which is exciting for a British person.

Texas is such a vast place, and the music seems to reflect that—it has this open spaciousness, and when you first hear it, the arrangements seem quite simple, but it has these very emotional, almost melodramatic qualities that are reflected in the color and vibrancy of a lot of the decorations and murals, and the bright awnings on the shops.

In the 1920s, San Antonio became one of the regular stops for the record company scouts, and they recorded all kinds of music there—country fiddle bands, and blues singers, and Western swing, and of course the Mexican American music was a big part of that. In 1928, Tommy Rockwell came there to do some sessions for OKeh Records, and he put ads in the local Spanish-language newspapers, inviting people to come and audition.

LYDIA MENDOZA: We were living there in Kingsville [Texas]. One day Papá was reading *La prensa*, the Spanish-language newspaper from San Antonio, and when he turned to the page that had the *aviso clasificado*, the classified ads, he exclaimed, "We're going to San Antonio!"

"What, Pancho?" Mamá asked him. "What are you talking about . . . ?"

It was then that he read us the advertisement. The OKeh record company announced that it was going to be recording Spanish-language musicians in San Antonio for two weeks. They wanted anybody that knew how to sing and play instruments. As soon as Papá saw that ad, he was convinced that we had to go straight to San Antonio.

Papá asked this man he knew in Kingsville if he could take us to San Antonio. You see, we didn't have any way to get there: no transportation or anything. This man had an old Dodge, [with] those skinny little tires like they used to have, and he had about twenty flats on that trip. . . . We would go for a few miles, and then we'd get another flat. We'd have to stop, and they would get out and raise up the car with a jack, and Papá would take off the tire, and they would put another patch on it. It took us two days to get to San Antonio, and it's only about one hundred and fifty miles. . . .

After we had auditioned, and they had decided that they liked the way we sang, we were told through their interpreter that they were going to give us $140 for twenty songs—that is, for ten records—and that they would pay for our trip to San Antonio. . . . The truth is that they paid us very little, but what did we know about these things? To us, $140 was a fortune. But the big thing, what we were really happy about, was that we got the chance to record, that they accepted us. The amount they paid us wasn't really that important; what we were after was a beginning, a start.[*]

ROGER HERNANDEZ: They were a traveling troupe, like a vaudeville act you could say. And they all played a musical instrument, whether it be the triangle, a bell, to a mandolin, to a violin, to a guitar. They all picked up a musical instrument and traveled like gypsies from town to town.

ANN HERNANDEZ-McKINNEY: It was their work, their way of living—

ROGER HERNANDEZ: —of surviving the tough times. So I figure it just all fell into place for the family, them being in show business, and it worked for them. They had the talent, which they were very fortunate to have realized and followed through with it, knowing that they could make a living off of it, and they did.

ANN HERNANDEZ-McKINNEY: In 1934, the family went and played at the Plaza del Zacate, in downtown San Antonio, and a gentleman by the name of Manuel Cortez happened to be dining there and heard [Lydia's] voice. He immediately was drawn to that, so he talked with her and invited her to go on a local radio station. And the people just went bananas when they heard her—a couple of songs were played, and the phone at the station was getting calls about her, and they wanted more.

---

[*] All Lydia Mendoza quotations are from Lydia Mendoza with Chris Strachwitz and James Nicolopulos, *Lydia Mendoza: A Family Autobiography* (Houston: Arte Público Press, 1993).

*Plaza del Zacate, San Antonio,
where Lydia was discovered*

ERA UNA CHIQUILLA TODAVÍA,

CUANDO TÚ CASUALMENTE ME ENCONTRASTE,

Y A MERCED A TUS ARTES DE MUNDANO,

DE MI HONRA EL PERFUME TE LLEVASTE.

LUEGO HICISTE CONMIGO LO QUE TODOS

LOS QUE SON COMO TÚ CON LAS MUJERES,

POR LO TANTO NO EXTRAÑES QUE YO AHORA

EN TU CARA TE DIGA LO QUE ERES:

MAL HOMBRE,

TAN RUIN ES TU ALMA QUE NO TIENE NOMBRE.

ERES UN CANALLA, ERES UN MALVADO,

ERES UN MAL HOMBRE.

[I WAS STILL A LITTLE GIRL WHEN YOU MET ME BY CHANCE,

AND THANKS TO YOUR WORLDLY ARTS, YOU TOOK AWAY
THE PERFUME OF MY HONOR.

THEN YOU DID TO ME WHAT ALL MEN LIKE YOU DO TO WOMEN,

SO DON'T BE SURPRISED THAT I NOW TELL YOU TO YOUR FACE
WHAT YOU ARE:

BAD MAN, YOUR SOUL IS SO VILE THAT THERE IS NO NAME FOR IT,

YOU ARE A WRETCH, YOU ARE AN EVILDOER,

YOU ARE A BAD MAN.]

—LYDIA MENDOZA, "MAL HOMBRE," 1934

*Lydia recording "Mal Hombre" at the
Texas Hotel, San Antonio, 1934*

ROGER HERNANDEZ: After the public heard her on the radio, Bluebird Records picked her up and wanted her to record. So she did a two-hour set and recorded eleven songs, with her first song being "Mal Hombre," which became her most popular and well-known song—that became her trademark. . . . She found a gum wrapper, and it was "Mal Hombre," and that's where the lyrics came from, and she made that her song. . . .

LYDIA MENDOZA: They used to print the lyrics of popular songs on gum wrappers there in Mexico. Every time you bought a piece of chewing gum, you had the chance to get a new song. I made a collection of many songs; and, of course, I didn't know the music to most of them. But I was interested in keeping them in case someday I might hear one of those songs. And I remember that I only heard the music to "Mal Hombre" once. One time a variety show came from Mexico City. There was a girl, a very pretty girl, in that show, and she sang tangos. . . .

When they announced "Mal Hombre," I became very excited. I was always very alert for the names of my songs. Wherever we went—I don't know why—I carried around that repertory just in case I heard them . . . and when she said "Mal Hombre," I got out the paper, the gum wrapper. I had it with me. And I just heard the music to that song that one time, but I memorized it. As soon as I got home I began to practice it and go over it, and it stuck with me.

ANN HERNANDEZ-McKINNEY: It's about an evil man who has broken her heart, and that touched a lot of hearts out there. It was a very popular tune with a lot of us women, of course.

ROGER HERNANDEZ: In the Hispanic-Mexican culture, it was hard for a woman to stand on her own, and she spoke of the struggles that women had in that time, that era, and she had the power and the voice to speak for them. That song was big, I think, for that reason—aside from it being a great tune and song in itself, it said a lot for women at that time. And if anything, I hope she helped one woman that was going through those struggles that are defined in that song to break away from whatever she was going through with her husband or whoever it was.

LYDIA MENDOZA: The first impression that I felt when my first recording came out was that I had made a mistake. "Now they won't come to listen to me in person," I said to myself. . . . "Who is going to come to hear me if they already have the record?"

And of course it was completely to the contrary. . . .

We had a little wind-up Victrola. As soon as the first record came out, my father became my first booster, and he advertised my record. There wasn't a house that he didn't stop at: "My daughter recorded, Lydia Mendoza recorded! Do you want to hear her?"

He would put the record on right then and there. And as soon as the people heard it, they would buy it.

ROGER HERNANDEZ: She played all through the Valley. Whatever little town we went through, Mom would remember, "Oh, that's where Grandma sang!" Or, "Grandma played at that little place there."

ANN HERNANDEZ-McKINNEY: Little theaters, like in Alice, Texas. As we traveled, she would always recall in all the little—

ROGER HERNANDEZ: Playing in all the little towns.

ANN HERNANDEZ-McKINNEY: That was her comfort zone.

ROGER HERNANDEZ: We used to sit down in a cafeteria or wherever, and here comes the people—they want her autographs or things like that, asking, "Oh, Lydia, you're here! When are you gonna play?"

"Tonight."

And, sure enough, they'd be there.

ANN HERNANDEZ-McKINNEY: She did everything on her own. She traveled all over the world by herself, just with her voice and her guitar, and her little amp.

ROGER HERNANDEZ: She was a very strong performer. She didn't need a whole lot of hoopla, backup, accompanists, extra instruments. Her voice just touched that thing in people's ears. She had that raspy, strong voice, and she had a vibrato that was her own, and it was catchy and very recognizable.

In 1999, Lydia received the National Medal of Arts from President Bill Clinton and Hillary Clinton, and was applauded by Aretha Franklin

ANN HERNANDEZ-McKINNEY: In her later years she was getting very well recognized for all that she has contributed to the culture. That's why she was awarded the highest achievement in the arts, the [National Medal of Arts] from the president of the United States. We were so excited about that—

ROGER HERNANDEZ: I personally kept an archive of all the items that Mom and Grandma got from the White House, from the invitation with the presidential seal from Clinton to the dinner menu. . . . I remember Mom coming back and telling us the stories of where they stayed, and all the private dinners that they went to. But for Grandma it was like "Oh, another." Like it didn't faze her, the significance of what she was getting, you know? It was just something that she did every day of her life. She appreciated it, but she wouldn't make such a big deal about it the way other people—

ANN HERNANDEZ-McKINNEY: Grandma was a very humble woman.

ROGER HERNANDEZ: That was part of her beauty. We'd go into the restaurants and people would stop by the table, and they were like "Lydia Mendoza! Lydia—" And they would get a napkin, and she would kindly sign her autograph. And for us it was like "Wow, people are coming to the table! How cool! They know Grandma!"

But for her it was just *"O, pues, es entendido. Que me conocen."* ["Oh, well, that's how it is. They know me."] She was just Lydia. It was her thing, and that was it. But for us, sitting on the outside looking in, it was a big thing. That's why I still want to make her legacy known, for the younger generations to know the importance of what she did for them.

ANN HERNANDEZ-McKINNEY: What she did for the music, but also for the people. Because it's not just picking up the guitar and playing, but it's what you are communicating from that to the people.

We are a strong family, we are a strong culture altogether, and that's what she stands for, in the message that she has delivered, and that's why it's important for us to keep that alive.

The U.S. Postal Service honored Lydia Mendoza with a commemorative stamp in 2013, hailing her as one of "the legends responsible for making American music part of global popular culture"

ROGER HERNANDEZ: They used to call her "*la cancionera de los pobres*," which was "the singer of the poor"—she spoke and sang for what people were thinking and living at that time. And a majority of that was the poor people, the migrant workers. She was their voice, so they named her as their singer, as their interpreter, as their message giver, for what was going on in their lives.

Hopefully somebody will learn and maybe take up on that. . . . Knowing that the times are so much different now than they were then, and that if she could have done it then, it's a thousand times easier to do it now—especially for a woman, 'cause she opened that door. And that it's never too late, and that nothing is impossible.

ANN HERNANDEZ-McKINNEY: Like right now, we're looking at each other, like, "Really?! Did that really happen?"

ROGER HERNANDEZ: It sounds like we're talking about somebody else that's on TV, but it's—

ANN HERNANDEZ-McKINNEY: It's our own grandmother.

ROGER HERNANDEZ: —what we grew up with, and not many people can say that. It's an amazing journey.

She lived to the age of ninety-one. She lived a good, long life, and loved her family deeply, and we were all thankful for the time that we had with her. And we always will be sad that she's gone, but, you know, she's not really gone. Because her music is with us, she's in our heart, and her legacy will live on.

This is a
Columbia
New Process
RECORD

Columbia
Viva-tonal   Recording
Columbia
ELECTRICAL PROCESS
Vocal Arcadian French Song
LAFAYETTE
(Allon a Luafette)
JOSEPH F. FALCON
15275-D
(146217)
MADE AND PAT'D IN U.S.A. JAN. 21, '13 AND RE. 16589
© COLUMBIA PHONOGRAPH COMPANY, INC., NEW YORK, U.S.A.

BIA New Process Records are ... mination of many years of ... nce and experiment. They ... highest achievement in record ... being free from distracting ... . They are the *only* records ...

worth while music is record-... bia Records, from the latest ... uring works of the immor-...

PHONOGRAPH COMPANY, INC.

tals. All recordings are by ar... tions recognized as finished ... that particular style of music ...

"Patented in U. S. A. as per data on r... countries, as follows: Canada, 1908—... 1911; 147504, 147505 and 147866-1918,... and 192108-1923—Austria, O.P. No. 58... 1918-17360; Feb. 2, 1918-17361; Mar. 4... 1919-17363—Argentine, 18101, Sept. 4... 11615-1921—France, Brevette S. G. D. ... 231346; 374519—New Zealand, A...

10   *ALLONS À LAFAYETTE*: THE BREAUX FAMILY

Joe Falcon and Cleoma Breaux on their wedding day

BERNARD: I fell in love with music from Louisiana when I was thirteen. The older brother of one of my friends had *Crawfish Fiesta* by Professor Longhair, and I was absolutely smitten by that record. Through that I got into Fats Domino and Huey "Piano" Smith, then the Meters, the Wild Magnolias, and that made me want to explore earlier Louisiana music. I discovered "Blues de Voyage," by the black Creole accordionist Amédé Ardoin, and the very first Cajun recordings, by Joe Falcon and Cleoma Breaux, and then her brothers, who recorded the song that became "Jole Blon," the most famous Cajun song of all time.

There was a great wave of international interest in Cajun music in the 1980s and '90s, and one evening I went to see the Lil' Band O' Gold, a Cajun rock band, at the Shepherd's Bush Empire in London, and was introduced to Pat Breaux, who played the saxophone and accordion. I asked him, "You're not by any chance related to the Breaux family that made those records in the '20s?" And he said, "Yes, Amédée Breaux was my grandfather."

Amédé Ardoin

We struck up a friendship, and when I began working on *American Epic*, he was one of the first people I called. It was a fortunate coincidence, because the Breaux family was absolutely central to the story of early Cajun recording. Amédée Breaux was one of the great accordion players, and his sister, Cleoma, played guitar with him, and then she married Joe Falcon, who made the first Cajun record, and she also played with Amédée and their brother Ophy on "Ma Blonde Est Partie," which became "Jole Blon," and then Amédée and Ophy recorded with a third brother, Clifford, as the Breaux Frères.

Pat's brothers Jimmy and Gary are also musicians, and their cousin Jerry Mouton is the family historian, so I had the idea of filming them together as a modern Breaux Frères. Pat said that might be a little complicated, because they didn't always get along, but he went to work on it, and we finally got them all around a table in this lovely old house in Vermilionville, a historic park near Lafayette, and it was an amazing experience. At one point, Jerry reached into this suitcase that had been sitting by his side and pulled out an accordion and put it on the table, and it was one of Amédée's accordions from the 1920s, and then he brought out Ophy's fiddle, and even the *'tit fer*, the metal triangle they used for percussion. They picked up the instruments and began playing, and it was absolutely magical: the descendants of the earliest recording artists playing their grandparents' music on the original instruments. It was like going back in time.

They started telling stories about Amédée—they called him "Papap 'Médée"—and his brothers, and clearly these artists are remembered as more than just musicians; they are local legends.

PAT BREAUX: Papap 'Médée, he was invited to an accordion contest, and it was against another young man, a black man I believe. The black man played his accordion, just played his song. It came to Amédée going—they were in a big barn—and he climbed up and went on the rafters and walked across the rafters of the barn, and played "Allons à Lafayette" while he was walking across the rafters. So, needless to say, he won the contest.

JERRY MOUTON: The antics they would do in some of those dances was kind of funny, and I guess probably they was under the influence of whatever beverage it was in those days—what I remember, it was supposed to have been white lightning or moonshine. But he got to feeling real good, and he kind of showed off his acrobatic skills by playing the accordion and he'd jump over the accordion [while he was playing], play behind his back, and then jump back around. And of course the crowd would go wild and everything. And of course the more libations he

Amédée Breaux (left, with accordion) *with friend*

Ophy Breaux

Clifford Breaux

had, I guess the control over his body wasn't as good, because sometimes he'd step right in the middle of the bellows.

So he'd come in at night from the dance and he'd throw that accordion in the trash, and my father would always go retrieve it and fix it up for him so he could play his next dance.

PAT BREAUX: Yeah. And he told us that that's how your daddy learned how to make accordions—

Fanny Marceaux, Joe Falcon, and Amelia Falcon

Amédée Breaux

Cleoma Breaux

Wade Mouton with handmade accordions

JERRY MOUTON: Yeah, that's exactly right. My dad learned how to make accordions, and he did that the rest of his life. He was a craftsman, thanks to Papap 'Médée. . . .

Papap was something else. Sometimes he didn't want to go home when the dance was over, you know. So in those days it was the Breaux Brothers and his sister Cleoma, they would play their dance, and coming back home, he didn't want to go home. So what they would do— Clifford and Ophy were pretty big men, they were six-footers, and Papap 'Médée was five-three, five-four maybe, at the most—so they'd hold Papap on the porch, they'd sit on him while Aunt Cleoma turned the car around and started driving away, and then they'd say, "Okay, let's go!" And they'd let him go and they would run and jump on the running boards of the car, and she would take off, leaving him behind.

And he would throw rocks and bricks and everything else, and the poor car was battered on the backside, you know. And then he'd sleep it off, and then the next day he wouldn't re-member anything.

PAT BREAUX: J. D. Miller, he had a recording studio in Crowley, and every time I went to re-cord over there, he'd tell me a story: he played with Amédée and the Breaux Brothers and he'd pick 'em up at their house; he had a Model T. He said from the moment he picked 'em up they fought—they fought there first, fought all through the gig—then, when they all would jump back in the car to go back home, everything was quiet—

JERRY MOUTON: You know, you hear the old stories about the dance halls, they had chicken wire around the band.

PAT BREAUX: I remember that—

JERRY MOUTON: It was supposed to keep the beer bottles from flying—

PAT BREAUX: To keep the band safe.

JERRY MOUTON: Yeah. But I think the chicken wire was there for the Breaux Brothers not to get to the audience. . . .

Papap 'Médée had so much rhythm; I mean he was *hopping*. He always played his accordion sitting down for the most part and he was just a-hopping and feeling the music. He was really one of the best I've seen, because he had a lot of soul.

It's amazing, coming from where he came from, a little old farming area in Branch [near Rayne, Louisiana]. Growing up in Branch, basically it was a community where they raised cotton and sugarcane and sometimes sweet potatoes. His daddy was, I guess, what you'd call a tenant farmer, and the old man, from what I heard, Grandpa August was even a better accordion player than Papap. I didn't meet August Breaux, but I did meet his wife, Papap's mom, [although] she couldn't speak English, so she wasn't somebody I could speak with. . . . She had Papap—he was the oldest—and then Uncle Clifford, and Uncle Ophy. And then came Cleoma. Now, that's a short period of time, because Clifford and Ophy, they were born eight months apart, you know, so that was pretty tough on Grandma Breaux.

Aunt Cleoma, she died at a very young age, but she had got with Uncle Joe Falcon and they started making their music together. So basically Aunt Cleoma left the Breaux Brothers and went with Uncle Joe. And what they did, they traveled together, and the different Breaux Brothers, they could all play all the different instruments. Normally, when they were traveling, Papap 'Médée played the accordion, Uncle Clifford played lead fiddle, Uncle Ophy played bass fiddle, and Aunt Cleoma played the guitar. Now when they split up—Aunt Cleoma went to Uncle Joe—well then, Uncle Ophy took the duty of playing the guitar. So that's how they ended up as the Breaux Brothers.

Cleoma Breaux and Joe Falcon

ALLONS À LAFAYETTE, MAIS POUR CHANGER TON NOM,

ON VA T'APPELER MADAME, MADAME CANAILLE COMME MOI.

PETITE, T'ES TROP MIGNONNE POUR FAIRE TA CRIMINELLE,

COMMENT TU CROIS QUE MOI, J'PEUX FAIRE, MAIS MOI TOUT SEUL?

[LET'S GO TO LAFAYETTE, TO CHANGE YOUR NAME,

WE'RE GOING TO CALL YOU MADAME, MADAME NAUGHTY LIKE ME.*

LITTLE GIRL, YOU'RE TOO CUTE TO ACT SO BAD,

HOW DO YOU THINK I'LL MAKE IT, IF I'M ALL ALONE?]

—JOE FALCON AND CLEOMA BREAUX,
"ALLONS À LAFAYETTE," 1928

BERNARD: It took a while for the record companies to get interested in Cajun music—at first they probably didn't even know it existed, and then the market would have seemed very limited. But in 1928, Frank Walker, a scout for the Columbia label, was doing some recording in New Orleans and decided to experiment.

FRANK WALKER: I happened to hear and know something of the story of the Cajuns, so I went up around Lafayette and through there over a weekend, and was astounded at the interest that there was in their little Saturday night dances. [They'd have] a single singer who'd have a little concertina type of instrument, and a one-string fiddle and the triangle. Those were the instruments . . . and, of course, they sang in Cajun. And to me it was funny, it had a funny sound. So I brought down a little group—I think his name, as I recall, was Joe Falcon; I brought him down to New Orleans and we recorded, just to have something different.

---

* Listeners disagree about whether Falcon sings "Madame Canaille *comme moi*" or "Madame Canaille Comeaux," and there is even a story that a woman named Comeaux threatened to sue him for defamation when the record came out.

JOE FALCON: George Burr, he took us in his car. He had a jewelry shop in Rayne, and he wanted to sell the record. . . . When he went to talk to them, they asked him where the band was, and he showed me and my wife and [Leon] Meche. In those days they wasn't making no records otherwise than big orchestra, you understand? They looked, and said, "That's not enough music." Said, "I can't use it."

Then Burr started talking again with him. . . . In his jewelry shop, on his book, he had 250 records was paid already—they wanted to be sure to have them, you understand? He said, "That man there's popular where I'm from in Rayne. Them people's crazy about his music and they want the record."

"Well," they said, "we don't know if it's going to sell." Then they turned around, they asked him, they said, "How much would you buy?"

He said, "I want five hundred, the first shot."

"Awww," they said, "five *hundred*? When you going to get through selling that?"

"Well," he said, "that's my worry, it's not yours. . . ." And he pulled out a blank check and he said, "Furthermore, make you a check for five hundred records."

They started looking at each other. "Well," they said, "you go ahead and play a tune just for us to hear." And it was all them stiff collars with coats on and everything, you know, them highfalutin. . . .

The one that was supposed to sing "Allons à Lafayette" was a man by the name of Leon Meche from Bosco, but he got all ready, button up his coat and this and that, and he was getting pale as a sheet, until he looked at me, he said, "You better sing that yourself. I might make a mistake. . . ."

So I opened that accordion, and it was a big building but it was close, and that thing was sounding like it wanted to take the roof off.

When I played that number they started talking to each other. They said, "Boy, that's more music out of two instruments than I ain't never heard in my life." They say, "Let's try one. . . ."

In those days them records was about a couple inch thick and you just could record on one side, you understand? It was wax, but you couldn't use those records to play on your Victrola, now; it was just to stamp the other records. They played it, and they all started going around the machine, all them highfalutin, they went around there and they listened, they listened. . . .

Boy, when they opened up the machine and it started singing and playing, you ought to see how I come for a chill, a goose bump—you know, I hear my own self singing. It make you feel kind of funny.

AND NOW IT IS HERE!

THE NEW

French Record

BY

Joseph F. Falcon

COLUMBIA RECORD
NUMBER 15031

Jones-O'Neal
FURNITURE COMPANY
YOUR CREDIT IS GOOD

435 Fifth St.
Phone 1066

516 Houston Ave.
Phone 1893

When the record got through playing, they walked back to me where I was recording, they said, "Partner, get ready. We're going for good now. We're going to make it."

FRANK WALKER: We put it on the market, we had tremendous sales . . . all over the state of Louisiana and some of Texas, because there was a great many of the Cajun people over in Texas. But it was amazing that you could sell fifty or sixty thousand records in a locality of that size.

JOE FALCON: I guarantee you, it made a hit for a while. You know, that was the first French record ever was recorded. That's why—because amongst your people, you know, if somebody do something that sounds good and everything, well, that's your own people, you force yourself like you want to get one, you understand? Even some of the poorest country fellows, they'd buy as high as two records. They ain't had no little Victrola, sure enough. Buy it and go to the neighbors and play it.

Cleoma Breaux and Joe Falcon with their daughter, Lulu

LOUIS MICHOT: "Allons à Lafayette" is a very quintessential Cajun song. It's about moving to the big town, Lafayette, and there's a lot of subcurrents in that song about, Do you want to be Cajun from a small town or do you want to go to Lafayette and change your name?

It became the hit of south Louisiana. My grandpa and my great-aunt used to tell me how, when they grew up in Mamou, they would hear that song coming out of the doors of these houses—everyone was so excited to have a Cajun song on record, because they had record players but there was no French music. When you grow up speaking French and all you listen to is English music, you know, you don't value your own music so much. When Cajun music comes out on a record, it gives you pride about your culture and about your music. So people were playing that record so often, they say you can't even find a record that still plays, because everyone who had one wore it out, because they loved it so much.

Joe Falcon (left)

Joe Falcon (far left) *with Clifford Breaux* (fiddle)

ALLISON: I had been to New Orleans before, but I'd never been to the Cajun country until our first research trip in 2006, and it's a very strange place: when you're driving along, looking out the window, it's really beautiful, with all these green trees and all this water—it looks just gorgeous. You don't realize that it's one of the hardest places in America to live, because there's no land to speak of, if you're in the bayou. The trees are just growing up out of the water, and you can't swim in the water because it's full of alligators, and there's the heat, and the mosquitoes.

We were talking with Louis Michot, who is a wonderful fiddler and singer with a younger-generation Cajun band called the Lost Bayou Ramblers, and he was very articulate about the land and its connection to the music.

LOUIS MICHOT: The bayous are very crooked and winding, like the music—we call it *croche*, that means "crooked," and it doesn't resemble any other music; it has its own cadence and its own rhythms and its own way of switching from chord to chord. It's very different, unfamiliar to the rest of America. The swamps are a pretty harsh place to live, and a lot of Cajuns went and settled on the prairie, a little calmer and flatter, but the music has always kept that intensity and that thickness of the swamps. It's a very dramatic landscape, where there's hurricanes always coming, there's giant rainstorms, harsh winters, and harsh summers. We're losing land all the time. There's definitely a sense of urgency in Cajun music, a sense of blues, and a joy from living where you love to live, but also a lot of suffering that goes along with it, because it's a very intense, harsh landscape.

Cajun music was more regional until Harry Choates brought out "Jole Blon" to the rest of the world [in 1946]. When "Jole Blon" became a national hit, that was really the first time that Cajun music entered the American mainstream. It became a hit that so many people covered—Moon Mullican, Roy Acuff, even all the way to Waylon Jennings and Bruce Springsteen. And Harry Choates got it from the Hackberry Ramblers, who got it from Leo Soileau, who got it from Amédée Breaux.

In 1929, Joe Falcon and Cleoma Breaux had their third chance to go record, in Atlanta, and that time Cleoma decided to bring her brothers Amédée and Ophy, and the three of them recorded "Ma Blonde Est Partie."

JOLIE BLONDE, 'GARDEZ DONC, QUOI T'AS FAIT,

TU M'AS QUITTÉ POUR T'EN ALLER.

POUR T'EN ALLER AVEC UN AUTRE, OUI, QUE MOI,

QUEL ESPOIR ET QUEL AVENIR MAIS MOI JE PEUX AVOIR...

JOLIE BLONDE, TU CROYAIS IL Y AVAIT JUSTE TOI,

IL Y A PAS JUSTE TOI DANS LE PAYS POUR MOI AIMER.

JE VAIS TROUVER JUSTE UNE AUTRE JOLIE BLONDE,

BON DIEU SAIT, MOI, J'AIME TANT.

[PRETTY BLONDE, JUST LOOK WHAT YOU'VE DONE,

YOU'VE LEFT ME TO GO AWAY.

TO GO AWAY WITH ANOTHER, YES, THAN ME,

WHAT HOPE AND WHAT FUTURE CAN I HAVE...

PRETTY BLONDE, YOU THOUGHT THERE WAS JUST YOU,

THERE'S NOT JUST YOU IN THE COUNTRY FOR ME TO LOVE.

I'LL FIND JUST ANOTHER PRETTY BLONDE,

GOOD LORD KNOWS, ME, I LOVE SO.]

—AMÉDÉE BREAUX, "MA BLONDE EST PARTIE," 1929

JERRY MOUTON: From what I remember, my grandmother was not a blonde, okay? And I think this is a song of an experience Papap 'Médée had with a young blonde, and she left him and it really tore him up. So these are memories he had.

GARY BREAUX: Yeah, all based on a broken heart. And this song is probably the most played Cajun song over the past years and to date.

PAT BREAUX: I don't know exactly when it came about, but all of a sudden you're hearing "'Jole Blon' is the Cajun national anthem."

JERRY MOUTON: Any musician that I run across, when I tell them it was my grandfather that made "Jole Blon," they've said, "Come on, are you kidding?"

And the only thing he got was—I think he sold the rights to a music company for eighty-something dollars back in the mid-'50s, was all he got. And in those days it was big money, you know? He thought it was big money.

PAT BREAUX: I heard that Cleoma actually wrote the words to "Jole Blon." I was told by another relative of ours; I was asking how "Jole Blon" came about, you know, and he told me Amédée couldn't write, so she'd write the words out for him.

JERRY MOUTON: Aunt Cleoma, it's a shame that she didn't live very long, you know, because she was very talented—

PAT BREAUX: I've heard the story that they think she got poisoned—they were playing at a gig, and some jealous woman or somebody spiked her drink. And the other one was that she got dragged by a car, her sweater got caught on the car and dragged her a quarter of a mile or something, and she never recouped from it.

JERRY MOUTON: You know, in those days you just don't have the forensics that can check it out. So it's a mystery how she did pass on; different people have different ideas about it. But the one that stayed with the family more than anything was that they seem to think it was a jealous woman, because Aunt Cleoma in those days, you know, she was a singer and she wooed a lot of the guys in the audience, and so all it took was somebody to keep coming to the dance to see her, and maybe a jealous wife might have done her in. But who knows; it's all speculation now.

Cleoma Breaux

Ophy, Amédée, and Clifford Breaux

LOUIS MICHOT: Cleoma Breaux was an amazing guitar player. She had a very solid, driving rhythm, which really supported the accordion, and Joe Falcon was an amazing accordion player who learned from her brother Amédée. "Falcon" was a Canary Island name—we call it *Isleño* [Spanish immigrants who came to Louisiana from the Canaries in the 1700s]. They moved to near Roberts Cove, which was a German settlement north of Rayne. Joe Falcon actually spoke three languages: he spoke French, English, and Spanish; and I've heard that his dad spoke five languages: Spanish, French, English, as well as German and whatever Native American language was spoke around Roberts Cove.

In general, the stories I've heard of Amédée Breaux and his brothers, they liked to drink a lot and they liked to fight a lot. Cleoma and Joe became professional musicians; they played almost every night of the week. Her brothers had a harder time keeping it together.

JERRY MOUTON: They had basically grassroots-type work: Papap 'Médée was a plumber's helper—they said he was so good with a shovel that they called him a little dragline, because he'd just work and work, and wouldn't stop. Uncle Ophy, he ended up driving a bulldozer, so he did very well with that. And I think Uncle Clifford worked for the city, in maintenance.

GARY BREAUX: [Papap 'Médée] devoted his last few years to the Lord. He discontinued playing in clubs altogether. And he died in the church—

JERRY MOUTON: Yeah, he was doing the invitational hymn—he was actually playing the accordion, walking down the aisle—and he passed, he dropped dead in his tracks.

LOUIS MICHOT: Cajun music has always been passed down through the families. We learned it from our dad and uncles. Our grandpa played music, his dad played music.

PAT BREAUX: I've been through all different phases of the Cajun music. When I started playing [accordion] I was, like, six or seven years old, and I wouldn't play for kids my own age, 'cause they didn't like Cajun music. This was, like, in the '60s. They made me play in my classroom; I was, like, third or fourth grade, and the kids were "Awww . . ." I mean, they wanted the '60s rock 'n' roll. I wanted to be cool, you know—only the people older, like thirty on up, liked the Cajun music—so I started playing saxophone.

Amédée Breaux (accordion) and Ophy Breaux (guitar)

   Then around in the mid-'70s, Cajun music started coming back. Young people were liking it more, and it just kept on growing. Now kids of all ages, everybody's buying accordions, everybody's cousin has an accordion now.

GARY BREAUX: The Cajun music now, it's stepped up more than the traditional Cajun music. You have your traditional Cajun music that your older people have more preference to, and this modern Cajun music, this is what's made the transition with the younger generation. The popularity has grown tremendously in this area.

JERRY MOUTON: It's kinda like progressive country and Cajun.

GARY BREAUX: Right. But you've got to have your foundation. And Amédée was the foundation.

AVALON BLUES: MISSISSIPPI JOHN HURT

BERNARD: In a very real way, Mississippi John Hurt changed my life. When I was fourteen years old, I found a record of his recordings from 1928 in the library, on an obscure British label called Spokane. I was entranced by it, and then I found a copy of his *Last Sessions* LP in a secondhand store in Streatham, and that was the first time I ever owned a record by an elderly person.

There was one song in particular, called "Let the Mermaids Flirt with Me," with the lyrics: "When my earthly trials are over, cast my body out in the sea. / Save on the undertaker's bill, let the mermaids flirt with me." That just completely touched my soul. It felt like I had discovered another grandfather—his voice had this warmth and gentleness, almost like someone aurally patting you on the shoulder and whispering in your ear. I'd never experienced that sense of intimacy listening to a record, and that was the point at which I realized for the first time that there was music from way beyond my time, from my great-grandparents' time, that was every bit as powerful and emotional as what I was listening to on the radio. That record convinced me that there was another world out there—not just a musical world, but a world of experience.

When I began this project, I knew from the start that John Hurt had to be part of it, because I believe his music can connect with a new audience as profoundly as it did with me. I was looking for a way to approach his story, and I became acquainted with his granddaughter Mary Frances Hurt, who has created a museum in the cabin where he used to live and is organizing a music camp for children in his hometown of Avalon, Mississippi. When I met her and listened to her memories of him, it just reaffirmed all the feelings I had from his records.

MARY HURT: People knew him as Mississippi John Hurt, but to us he was Daddy John. He lived above the store, and he would be standing always by the mailbox, just like he was wait-

ing for somebody to come up the hill, and he always had this radiant smile. His smile was like a pebble thrown in the lake, and it would just spread. And he had the kindest eyes; his eyes spoke volumes. I didn't see any of the poverty or any animosity or any of the things that were depressing, ever, in his face. He transcended that—it was like it didn't exist to him.

I remember the local people on Saturdays, and after church on Sunday evening, they would gather around in his yard or 'round the old mulberry tree, and he would play for them. He played in all of the major events in the community, or he would go to the old depot in Carroll-ton and play for people to come. My aunt Fanny talked about how Daddy John would come to the school and they would have the school dances with his music.

When Daddy John was alive there were hundreds of families in this community, both African American and white—it's a ghost town now compared to the way that it was. As I walk through Avalon today, I can visualize the store and the cotton gin and the houses and the families that lived here, and the hill where Daddy John lived, and my dad, my mom—it's heartbreaking in a way. But this town existed. It was a real place, and real families, real people lived here. I have a very vivid snapshot in my heart, in my mind—and the only thing left of my childhood is his cabin.

JOHN HURT: I was born in Mississippi, Carroll County, in a place that they called Teoc, but they brought me away from Teoc when I was a small kid, and I was raised up near Avalon. I started playing guitar when I was eight years old—you might say I kind of stole my way of making music, in a way: there was a gentleman that would come to see a schoolteacher at the school I went to, William Henry Carson. He lived in Teoc, that's a good ways from Avalon, and he would come up every weekend to see this teacher, and he'd spend the night at our house; he'd come up on Friday and go home Saturday. He had a guitar, and he could play—I don't know how many numbers he could play, but I never heard him play but one, and he'd sit up there and play it for us, and I wanted to learn it awful bad. I wanted to learn to play guitar anyway—I always liked music.

He would set his guitar down, and by inching around, inching around, I'd get over there by it and pick it up. He said, "Uh-uh, son. Put that down."

My mother would speak up, say, "Yeah, put that man's guitar down!"

I'd say, "Yes, Mother," and put it down. And I studied me a sharp plan to get that guitar and try to learn it.

My mother said, "Aw, it's about time you go in the room and go to bed anyway."

"Yes, Mother." I'd get up and I'd go in the room and go to bed, but I wouldn't go to sleep. When they quit talking and go in their different rooms and go to bed, well, I'd lie there and listen, listen, listen. And way in the night, I figured they're asleep. I'd get up and I'd tip to my mother's room door and I'd listen. I could kind of hear her sleeping; I'd say, "Yeah, she's asleep." I'd go to this gentleman's room door and I could hear him good! [Mimics a man snoring.] I'd say, "Oh, yeah."

Then I would tip around and get his guitar. And I'd just [plays a few quiet notes], 'bout like this. And I kept doing that until I learnt that number. And when I'd learned to play that number good, why, I didn't care if he did hear me then.

I waked my mother one night about one o'clock, playing that number. She opened her room door and peeked in there. She says, "Bless my Lord, I thought that was William Henry!"

I said, "No, Mother, it's me." She stood there for a good little bit. I looked around, she kept standing there. I said, "And, Mother, I want you to buy me a guitar."

She said, "I haven't got anything to buy you no guitar."

So the white gentleman that she washed for, why, the next day was wash day and she were telling him about it. He says, "Why, Mary Jane"—that's my mother's name—says, "I can get him a guitar."

She said, "Mr. Kent, I'm not able to buy him no guitar."

He said, "How do you know?"

She said, "Well, I know I don't have nothing to buy a guitar. I haven't got anything." You could get a good guitar then for ten dollars.

He said, "Mary Jane," says, "I have a guitar that's practically new that my boy married off and left at home and he told me that I could have it. Said he didn't want it—sell it, or anything. I'll let you have that guitar for one dollar and a half." And she bought it. So I just kept going then.

BERNARD: John Hurt played a very varied mix of music, from popular ragtime compositions to ballads and country dance tunes, to his own compositions, which often showed a rather mischievous wit. One of the interesting things about his story is that, despite the harsh racial segregation, at times he played at local dances with a white fiddle player, and that was how he came to the attention of the record scouts for OKeh, Bob Stephens and Tommy Rockwell.

JOHN HURT: A gentleman at home, Willie Narmour, he was a fiddler, and he went to a fiddling contest in Winona, and he won the fiddling contest. Mr. T. G. Rockwell and Mr. Stephens were there at this fiddling contest, going through, searching for music, and they got after him to record some with them, and asked him if he knew anybody else in this country that made music.

He said, "Well, there's a colored fellow in my area, I think he plays the guitar mighty well." He says, "Which-a-way y'all going back to New York?" They told him, and he says, "Well, I'll tell you, it's not very much out of the way. Come on, go by the way of Greenwood. I'll take you to this colored fellow's house and let you hear him, see what you think about him." So they did.

They came there one night at one o'clock. Of course I knew Mr. Narmour, and he tapped on the door, and I said, "Who is that?"

He says, "Get up, John! Here's some people from New York, want to hear you play some."

I didn't say anything to him, but I just said in my mind, "Aww, Mr. Willie, now you just got some company, now you want me to get up and play. I know what, you have no men from New York."

Well, I got up and opened my door, and sure enough. I didn't know right then they *were* from New York, but I knew it was somebody that didn't live around there. They walked in,

spoke to me, and asked me if I had a guitar. I told them I did. He said, "Well, get your guitar and play me a piece."

I played him one, "Monday Morning Blues," started on another one, and he stopped me. He said, "That'll do, son. How about getting you to come to Memphis and record some?"

I told him, "I reckon it's all right."

He said, "Well, all right. Have you ever been to Memphis?" I told him I had once or twice. He said, "Well, here. I'm going to leave you a card here. You come to this building. I'm going to leave you a card and your train fare and everything." Says, "I'll depend on Narmour getting you to the train—Narmour, will you get him to the train?" Well, it wasn't far, I could walk to the train. But he promised him that he would. At that time, [Narmour] was driving the school bus, so he just brought his students to school and kept right on and picked me up, takin' me on to the train.

BOB STEPHENS: Tommy Rockwell and I were on our field trip to Memphis, where we already had some acts set up to record. In those days you'd take your recording equipment and your wax shaver, get a lot of rugs and pad the walls of the building you were recording in. Tommy told me he could take care of things and suggested that I take a trip down the Mississippi Delta and see what I could find in the way of Race stuff, then come back inland for hillbilly stuff. So I stopped in all the little towns and all the local record stores to see what was going on, and I wound up in Jackson, Mississippi, and I thought, "The hell with it, this is ridiculous!" So I saw the biggest dealer in town and suggested that we organize an old-time fiddling contest and the winners would get an OKeh contract. He thought it was a great idea and made signs and hung them up all over the county. Rockwell came down to judge, and a team named Narmour and Smith won. We brought them to Memphis to record and subsequently they came to New York.

While this was going on, we kept hearing about some wild blues singer named Mississippi John Hurt, so we set out to find him. The trouble we had! Finally, we tracked him down late at night. It was blacker than a whale's belly and we had to put the headlights onto the door of his shack before we knocked. This guy came to the door wearing just a pair of trousers and he damned near turned white when he saw us. He thought we were a lynching party.

MARY HURT: He was startled when they came to his house. He didn't know what had happened, because, for one thing, he wasn't sure whether they was looking for his brother Hennis, who was a notorious moonshiner—he was known to have the best moonshine in the county, and they were forever arresting him for that.

The McCall Building, Memphis, Tennessee, site of John Hurt's first recording session

BOB STEPHENS: We told him who we were and he asked us in. He threw a few logs on the fire and we saw his wife in a corner in a cot, and then he took out his guitar and starts to sing. He was great! So we booked him into Memphis. . . .

JOHN HURT: I goes to Memphis and made two records for him. Got back home, was at home one week, and he sent me a letter and my train fare in there to come to New York for further recording. . . . I never will forget, when he sent for me to come to New York, I met him in Memphis, and I told him, I said, "I certainly am glad to see you, Mr. Rockwell."

He says, "Why?"

I say, "I ain't gon' taking that trip by myself."

IIe says, "Ohhh." Says, "You gotta stay by yourself—I'm on my way to Dallas, Texas, 'cause we got some recording business out there."

So he went on that way, west, and I taken off for New York. . . . Asked me to come, bring them six selections, and I did do it: forty dollars a record, twenty dollars a side.

[There] was a record store in Greenwood, the nearest hometown, about ten or twelve miles from Avalon. So this record store man, he got lots of my records, and they just went like wildfire. The first ones he got I never will forget: I was working on a farm, after I went to record for the OKeh and I'd got back home. So he come to my home to get me to go down to his record store, to play some of those records, you know, what he was selling to people. . . .

So I went there and got to playing there. They're standing looking at me, they said, "Well, that sound just like him, too. Mmmm. I don't think this is Mississippi John. He can play those songs just *like* Mississippi John." And they didn't want to believe it. That's right. Said, "He sure play it just like him, but I don't know—I most believe that's him." But it certainly was. . . .

I never did hear any more from [OKeh] in a pretty good while, and when I did hear, why, they gone out of business. So then I wait for thirty-five years, and these people came along. . . .

BERNARD: OKeh released six records by Mississippi John Hurt in 1928 and 1929, but they had very limited sales, and by the mid-1930s Columbia Records discontinued the label. When Harry Smith released his six-LP anthology, *American Folk Music*, in 1952, he included two of Hurt's recordings, "Frankie" and "Spike Driver Blues," but Hurt sounded like one of the oldest performers on the set, and most listeners assumed he was long dead. Then in 1963 a record collector named Dick Spottswood heard a copy of Hurt's last OKeh release, on which he sang a song about leaving home to make that second recording trip to New York:

> *Been to New York this morning, just about half-past nine,*
> *I been to New York this morning, just about half-past nine,*
> *Thought of m'little mama in Avalon, couldn't hardly keep from cryin'.*
>
> *Avalon's my hometown, always on my mind,*
> *Avalon's my hometown, always on my mind,*
> *Pretty mama's in Avalon, want me there all the time.*
>
> *The train left Avalon, throwing kisses and waving at me,*
> *When the train left Avalon, throwing kisses and waving at me,*
> *"Just come back, daddy, stay right here with me . . ."*

New York's a good town but it's not for mine,
New York's a good town but it's not for mine,
Going back to Avalon, stay with pretty mama all the time.

—MISSISSIPPI JOHN HURT, "AVALON BLUES," 1928

DICK SPOTTSWOOD: I heard "Avalon Blues," heard Hurt singing, "Avalon's my hometown, it's always on my mind," and I went to an atlas to see if I could find a place in Mississippi called Avalon. It seemed like a no-brainer at the time, but it was a link in the chain, and such a place existed. When another friend, a young folk musician named Tom Hoskins, decided that he was going to go down to the Mardi Gras in New Orleans in 1963, I looked at the map again and I said, "It's not too far out of your way to stop by Avalon, Mississippi, and see if anybody has ever heard of John Hurt." He said, "No, why not?" So he did, and Avalon's a very small town—I think he was on Hurt's doorstep within ten or fifteen minutes.

JOHN HURT: About nine o'clock that night, Mr. Hoskins knocked on my door. I asked, "Who is that?"

He said, "Is this where Mississippi John Hurt lives?"

I thought it was someone nearby, so I said, "Yeah," and I opened the door and he walked in.

He looks at me and said, "John, have you got a guitar?" I told him I didn't have one and he said, "No sweat." He walked right out to his car and came back with a guitar and he said, "John, I want you to play this."

I thought the man was a sheriff or the FBI, and I was thinking to myself, "What have I done?" I hadn't done anything mean, and I knew he was after the wrong man and he wasn't looking for me.

Then he said, "John, we have been lookin' for you for a long time. I want you to come to Washington with me and make some records. Will you go?"

I said, "Yeah, I'll go. . . ."

DICK SPOTTSWOOD: I told Bill Clifton, who was on the board of directors at the Newport Folk Festival that year, and he told Pete Seeger. Pete Seeger knew who John Hurt was because of the Harry Smith anthology, [and] just insisted to the rest of the board up there—even though the schedule was officially closed and everything was sort of locked in already—he said, "You've got to find a place for this."

John Hurt was not only on the little schedule of workshops and things during the day, but they had him on the big evening concert, which was typically attended by five, ten, twenty thousand people. Nobody except for the record collectors knew who he was, but John Hurt was very lucky. John Hurt had—and it was just part of who he was—a very magnetic personality. He was a little elf. He didn't ask for attention or anything, but he knew what to do with it when he got it: it was just a kind of personal connection that I think everybody there felt. It was amazing! I mean, people knew that this was a great historical artifact—like having the Carter Family there for the first time, they represented a big slice of history—but John Hurt was also a hit.

MARY HURT: The Newport Folk Festival was an introduction to a side of a human being, through music, that just shocked people: here's this little statue of a man, and his gentleness and his touch was electrifying to the hearts of people who couldn't even speak the language, or understood even the culture of where this guy came from. But it just spoke to people from everywhere—it just opened up a whole different world to people.

Then he wrote home and said he was gonna be on this big television show, the Johnny Carson show, and it was a late-night show, and we didn't have a television. So Miss Annie Cook [a white neighbor] allowed everybody to come, and she had this television set, and everybody was there that could get in that little room. And when my daddy saw Daddy John played on television, I mean the expression on his face was like "This can't—I mean, how can this be?" It was—wow!—it was a wonderful moment in the community.

ALLISON: When we met Mary, we first visited at her home outside Chicago, and she was the most incredible woman. Her family has suffered so much, but she was so generous, and we bonded because her dream is to have a summer camp in Avalon where underprivileged urban kids could get away from the city and come there, and could learn music. And that meant a lot to me, because where I come from in Scotland there was a lot of poverty—nothing in comparison to what she went through in Mississippi, of course—and I was lucky enough to be given a clarinet, and music became like a safe haven for me; it changed my life.

When we met her again in Avalon, it was like this magical place, with birds and insects and fireflies. We arrived at John Hurt's cabin, which she's moved to this lovely clearing in the woods, and it was simply crawling with ladybugs, which we consider lucky in Britain. And the way she talked about him, and her family, and the music, a lot of it was painful, but it was also like something out of a fairy tale.

Taj Mahal and John Hurt, Newport Folk Festival, 1964

Annie Cook

Mary Hurt

MARY HURT: My father was always sick; I never remember him all of my life being well. When Daddy John left, Daddy's illness was very apparent to us, and Daddy John promised him it was just gonna be for a little while, but he would be back, and he would be in touch. . . . But my dad got very sick one day, and it was the first time he ever had stayed in a hospital, and probably about noon my mother came home and she had my father's shoes and his pants and his shirt folded very neatly in her arms. And when she got out of the car she just collapsed and she said, "Your daddy's gone, he's gone."

I think there is that one thing that God created you for, and you're not whole until you complete that. And I truly believe in my whole heart that Daddy John, when he made the decision to leave his sick son, to go away, to lead a life that he had no idea about and go into a whole world different than he ever knew before—it was greater than a quest. And when he came back

for my dad's funeral, he had done everything that he needed to do, or fulfilled his purpose in this life. It was such a dark, dark time, like somebody came in and just turned the lights off in my life. And Daddy John came home, and he assured my mother, "Don't worry, 'cause I'm gonna be here."

I remember before my dad's funeral, someone coming and telling Daddy John that he had a performance he was scheduled to do. And he said, "No, I can't go anymore, I can't." And that's really the first time that I'd ever seen a glimmer of anger or sternness, and it was like—it wasn't mean, but it was a voice that I had never heard before; he said it with such defiance. And he didn't leave anymore.

You know, two things I never saw Daddy John do: I never saw him without his hat and I never known him to drive. And it was amazing to me, because my father had this fanaticism about cars and driving, and Daddy John would watch him work on cars and he was fascinated, but I never saw him even ask to drive, you know. But at my dad's funeral, Daddy John insisted on leading the hearse up the hill to bury my father—he told my mother, "Okay, I'm going to take you guys up there, and we're gonna properly put him away, and you just follow along." So the hearse was following along up the hill, and then at the very top of the hill the truck just cut off, it just died. And my brother-in-law, who was a mechanic, he got out and he tried to fix it, and he couldn't start it. And there was the hearse and all of these cars lining up and down this one little narrow road, and it was August, and it was very hot.

Daddy John got out of the truck, and he told my brother-in-law to stay in the truck, and he said for us to be quiet. I remember him walking into the center of the road, and for the first time in my life I saw Daddy John take off his hat. He held it to his chest, and he looked up in the sky and he said, "T.C."—that was my father's name—"T.C., I know it's you. And it's gonna be all right. I'm gonna take care of Ann and I'm gonna help her with the kids. Now I need you to do something for me. I got your babies here in the back of this truck, and I need to go up here now and let them give you a proper good-bye."

And he looked up in the sky, and suddenly this wide grin that I was so used to came over

his face, and he put back on his hat and he said, "Much obliged." And he jumped back in the truck and told my brother-in-law, he said, "Louis, hit it." And that truck started instantly, and it went up that hill, and it never stopped again.

This cabin and these woods, this place is where he loved: just the simplicity of all of it, the sounds, the beauty of all of this. The day Daddy John had his stroke, he was exploring these woods; he came early one morning, in the dawn of the morning, and he walked the woods with his shotgun. Because it was fall, he was squirrel hunting, and as he was hunting, he had a stroke. He was unconscious, with the gun across his lap, and he never recovered. And I would say it was a tragedy, but he died the way he loved. And he's buried in this place, his home. Daddy John's home.

JOHN S HURT
BORN MAR 8 1892
DIED NOV 2 1966

Mary Hurt

12 | THE *AMERICAN EPIC* SESSIONS

★ ★

BERNARD: As we traveled in the footsteps of the early record scouts, we often felt that we were having similar experiences and making similar discoveries. Visiting the communities and meeting the families of musicians we had known only from old recordings, what had begun as an exploration of the past became a way of exploring and understanding the present. The music provided us with a deep connection to modern people and places, just as it connected those people to their own history and culture, and we increasingly felt as if we were engaged in an ongoing process: the first burst of regional recording allowed Americans to hear one another across boundaries of space, culture, and language, and now lets us hear and connect across time.

That was a very powerful feeling, but it also made us hungry to know more about the actual process of making those recordings—how the scouts, producers, and engineers captured the sounds that survive today, and what it was like for the musicians to be confronted with this new technology. So we were always looking for pictures or films of recording sessions, or simply of the recording equipment, and no matter how hard we tried, we kept coming up blank. I couldn't understand it, and I started asking everybody I knew who was interested in this period, but nobody could recall seeing a picture of the actual recording apparatus. That seemed like a huge missing piece of the puzzle, and also a mystery—this technology was so important, and was used in thousands of recording sessions all over the country, often with major stars, so why were there no photographs?

Eventually, I was talking with Michael Kieffer about this, and he told me about a guy in Los Angeles named Nick Bergh who was researching early recording technology. I went to see Nick, and he explained that the lack of photographs was not accidental: the early recording companies were worried that competitors would copy their equipment, so they were very wary of having it documented.

*Nick Bergh, recording engineer who rebuilt the
Western Electric recording system*

NICK BERGH: The secrecy came from the acoustic era. It's relatively complicated to make the equipment to do acoustic recordings, but not that complicated. A good analogy would be something like Coca-Cola, where all the ingredients are available but it took thousands of hours to put them together and mix them right. That's why they had to be so guarded with it, because anyone could get their hands on a recording diaphragm or the pieces to make something—the problem was how to hook everything together and adjust it just right. So they were very secretive, and there are even stories about engineers taking recording heads home with them so they wouldn't be left in the building overnight.

When they moved into the electric era, they just continued that tradition. It wasn't necessarily the manufacturers—Bell Labs or Western Electric—that were being secretive about it, it was the record companies. But the result is that today it's almost like this whole era didn't exist, because there is so little in the way of pictures or documentation. We were able to locate two motion pictures, one from His Master's Voice in 1927 and the other from Columbia in 1928, but they show mostly the microphone and the head on the lathe. As far as the amplifiers go, they're still very careful about hiding those in the shadows or just showing them for a second, so you get a glimpse but can't see what is actually happening.

BERNARD: The first time I went over to Nick's house he was very friendly, and he showed me a wax cake like they used to use for master recordings, and then he brought out this little wooden box with a Western Electric cutting head resting in it, sort of like a severed monkey's paw. I was thinking, "If he has this, there has to be more." So at one point I asked him if he had a workshop, and he said, "Yes, but you can't come in there. I'm working on a secret project." I had no idea what that might be—I actually thought it might be something for the government—and that seemed to be all I could learn from him.

I went on with my investigations and eventually came up with some blurry pictures of recording activity, but you couldn't really see anything. It was very frustrating, because for that key period in the late 1920s all the major record companies were using the same Western Electric recording system, and I wanted to be able to show what it was like. I kept asking historical audio experts—I spoke with Duncan Miller in Britain, who had worked on rebuilding an acoustic recording apparatus for EMI—but nothing was working out. So eventually, a year or two later, I called Nick again and said, "We were wondering if somehow, by any chance, you knew where one of these machines might be."

There was a long pause, and then he said, "I've rebuilt one."

NICK BERGH: My initial attempts to put together the Western Electric system were largely hopeless, since all the information I could find was incomplete and often intentionally misleading, to protect against competition. The break came from my research in early motion picture sound: although almost all of the music studio equipment from this time had been destroyed, there were a few pieces that survived because they were used for motion picture and early broadcast use, where the Western Electric system continued to be licensed decades after the music studios had stopped using it.

It took over a decade to finally piece the system together. All the individual items had to come from different places, often thousands of miles apart—a couple pieces even came from Japan. I was able to confirm my progress by studying the few crude music studio pictures and films that started to turn up, and from the coded information on original recording ledger sheets. Although each of these sources was ambiguous or misleading on its own, together they confirmed what was actually being used, and the system finally became fully operational in 2012.

BERNARD: The astonishing thing was that Nick had actually rebuilt an authentic Western Electric recording system—not a replica but the real thing, from original parts. It was a hugely

Scully lathe, circa late 1920s

important accomplishment, because although this equipment was only used for a few years, it formed the blueprint for all later sound technology. That system was one of the jewels of the early industrial age. It was really expensive, and there seem to have been only between one and two dozen machines making all the recordings in America at that time. Western Electric retained ownership of them and leased them to the record companies. That was one of the reasons so little was known about them, but also meant that the equipment was extraordinarily well made.

NICK BERGH: This was essentially developed by the phone company, and they were interested in building things that didn't break down, because they leased everything, so it cost them less money to overbuild things and not to have to send out service people to go up to the top of a power pole or something. Even the tubes were leased—you couldn't go to your local electronics store and buy a Western Electric tube; you had to be RCA Victor or Columbia or Warner Brothers. So they could make everything to a quality that wasn't necessarily commercially viable—if you want to fix a guitar amplifier from the '50s, you normally have to replace the capacitors, but the capacitors and the coils in this equipment were made to never fail, so they are still mostly good today.

Western Electric voltmeter measures current for power supply

BERNARD: Nick had also found a weight-driven cutting lathe, but it was from a somewhat earlier period, so at that point we got in touch with the Scully family, who had been the main manufacturers of recording lathes throughout the twentieth century. I went to visit them, and asked if they had any photographs or film footage, and they said they didn't. However, they added, "We do have a lathe." They took me down to a basement, and there, gleaming with all its chrome, was a 1924 lathe that Jerry Scully's grandfather had made—probably the only one still in existence.

ALLISON: Once we had the equipment sorted out, I began looking for a studio we could use. I tried the usual recording studios, but none of them seemed right—for one thing, you need quite special acoustics for this machine, and also we were going to be filming the sessions, so we needed space to move the cameras, for the dolly and the film crew. Eventually, someone told me about an old studio on Melrose, opposite Paramount Studios, which had been around since

The first American Epic *session with Frank Fairfield*

the 1930s—it was just being used as storage space, but it had been a quite important location, where people like Count Basie and Duke Ellington recorded, and we went to look at it, and it was perfect.

BERNARD: Our original idea was to film a typical 1920s recording session, so I got in touch with Frank Fairfield and the Americans—who play very much in the style and spirit of that period—and with T Bone Burnett providing production advice, we filmed a number of songs. It was like a séance, communing with the musical ghosts of the past through this equipment that had not been used in almost ninety years—it felt like the echoes of Bessie Smith, Louis Armstrong, and Jimmie Rodgers were still flowing through the wires. And the sound was amazing: clear and punchy, but utterly different from a modern recording.

By that time it was obvious that this should be more than just a footnote to our historical explorations, so we sent a clip of the Fairfield session to Jack White, and he agreed to team

"When they look down on hip-hop music because of the words that were used and stuff like that, it didn't start with hip-hop. It started a long time ago. It started with America." —Nas

Jack White

up with T Bone and produce a whole series of recordings. Jack seemed like the perfect person, because he loves old records and old technology, but he is also a modern performer and is in touch with people who are doing innovative work in all sorts of styles. We didn't want the feeling of this just being a historical reenactment—we wanted to recapture the spirit of that first wave of regional recording, when all kinds of different artists, playing a mix of traditional material and current compositions, were confronted with this unfamiliar technology.

In that spirit, it was important that we include a broad range of music—we wanted to record country and blues, but also a Hawaiian group and a Cajun band, and some more contemporary artists, and I had some dream projects, like getting the Mexican star Ana Gabriel to sing Lydia Mendoza's "Mal Hombre." We were looking for people who had a certain purity to them, who would be capable of delivering powerful, self-contained, emotional performances in just a few takes, and who would be sensitive to the uniqueness of the situation. And we wanted to have some surprises, some people you would not normally think of in this context—for example, we wanted to have a rapper, and were very fortunate to get Nas.

At first we thought it might be hard to find contemporary artists who would want to record with this ancient technology. But when I first went to see T Bone, he happened to be producing a record with Elton John, and when I'd finished presenting the project, Elton looked at T Bone and said, "You should produce this," and T Bone said, "Yeah, I'd love to," and then Elton said, "You probably won't want an old queen like me on this, but if you do, I'm here to do anything you'd like." That was quite a vote of confidence, so we got together with Jack and T Bone and made a list of about twenty artists we would like to have, and virtually all of them said yes.

JACK WHITE: I think a lot of us who've loved so much music that's been recorded in this time period, the '20s and '30s, always wondered what it would be like if we could record our songs in this way. And it really does change your perspective. . . . I love the looks on people's faces when they first hear the playback from the record, because it's the first time they've ever heard that done with their own voice, and it's like the first time a child hears his voice played back on a tape recorder.

It's strange at first, because it doesn't sound like a digital recording, which is very similar to what actually occurred in the room—there's frequencies that aren't there for modern recording, and you're dealing with hearing the vibrations out of a mechanical object, not the digital ones and twos of computer recording, or even a tape recording. This is an actual physical, mechanical means by which you are reproducing the sound, and that colors the sound in a beautiful way. It really has its own life to it.

The Hawaiians: Bobby Ingano, Auntie Geri, and Charlie Oyama

Taj Mahal with Karl "Fats" Kaplin, Dominic Davis, and Patrick Ferris

Raphael Saadiq with Lillie Mae Rische, Daru Jones, and Fats Kaplin

"*American Epic is more than a music documentary. This is history. It's had such an incredible impact on so many people.*" —Elton John

The Americans and Ashley Monroe

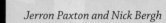

Jerron Paxton and Nick Bergh

Bettye LaVette and Bernard MacMahon

ANA GABRIEL: It was such an emotional experience—I think this is something I will bear with me, like a tattoo in my memory, in my breast. . . . I keep coming back to the word *magic*; it was magical. I was asking myself, "I'm going to record and at the same time my voice will be transmitted directly to the acetate?" There was a strong emotion, but also some doubt—and more so when I arrived and found that for the first time I would be singing without needing to use earphones. It is such a pure way of recording. . . . It's difficult for me to express how this feels.

Ana Gabriel

JACK WHITE: I think every artist needs to experience recording like this at some point in their lives, because you have to conform to the machines, they're not going to conform to you. In modern recording, you go into a studio and we put the mic as close as we want to you, and we put a compressor on it, and we EQ it and alter it in all these ways to conform to who you are. But this style of recording changes people's characters: it makes them sing quieter or louder, with an accent or non-accent, stressing certain syllables that you wouldn't normally do, so they get picked up on the recording.

That's an interesting bit of knowledge that I picked up from this—how it changes the character of the artist. A lot of the recordings we've loved for so long, we're hearing the results of them having to conform to this—they're not singing the way they would have normally, and I think that made for better results at times, because it pushes you to go to a place you never would have been before.

The problem with modern recording is that people get very used to the idea that they can fix it later, so they don't really put their all into their performance. Most of the great artists and the great records that have become so iconic and so important to the world were recorded in this fashion, where everyone had to have it rehearsed and perfected on their own before they even set foot in the studio. Modern musicians and bands don't have that pressure anymore, and they don't know what it's like, and it changes you as an artist—the performance happens in this one moment and it's finished; you don't remix, you don't overdub, you don't remaster. You have to have it exactly the way you'd hope for it to be immediately, live, while you're recording. When you get it right, it feels like an accomplishment, like you climbed a mountain. That's a great place to be—but it's also a scary place to be.

NAS: Recording this way is crazy, because it's one microphone picking up everything—if there's backup singers, they're really standing behind you and they're singing; if there's a band playing, the mic is picking up the lead vocalist, the background singers, and all the instruments. I'd never done anything like that, and it was hard to do, because you couldn't punch it in, you couldn't stop it at one word and then finish it up where I messed up at.

I enjoyed the idea of it, you know, preparing for it—but doing it was like real work, you know what I'm saying? At first I wanted to do an entire record this way, but it's not as easy as I thought it would be. I would need to spend a lot of time around this old equipment to really figure out how to get my sound off on it . . . 'cause right now I feel like Alexander Graham Bell is gonna come out of the speaker, you know? I can almost see the inventor's face, and I'm thinking about stuff like that more than making a song.

Director Bernard MacMahon's rough sketches for the lighting and set design of two scenes from the American Epic sessions.

*Los Lobos: César Rosas, Conrad Lozano,
Louie Pérez, and David Hidalgo*

"When you're recording there's so much time spent on the mix and all the work after you record it. To have your work all done, right there, it's a relief." —Beck

Lillie Mae Rische, Dominic Davis, Edie Brickell, Steve Martin, Fats Kaplin

BERNARD: It was a very challenging process, because these first electrical mics respond completely differently than contemporary microphones. They are extraordinarily sensitive to the proximity of the musicians and the singers, and also to where people are standing—the tiniest step to the left or right will radically alter the balance and tone of the instruments. One of the first hurdles to overcome was that musicians would listen to a playback of their recording and then try to adjust themselves as they would in a modern studio, which invariably made the mix sound worse.

JACK WHITE: Producing music in this style, you really have to interact with the artists and do your best to communicate to them exactly what's going on, because the microphone is completely stationary and the performers themselves are basically the faders—how close the mandolin player or the fiddle player is to the mic is almost like how much you would move your fingers on a fader to mix a song. That's a really interesting part of it, but sometimes I felt a little guilty about having to keep directing, saying, "I'm sorry, you have to turn your head sideways when you get to the chorus of the song or it distorts."

Like, Beck had a gospel choir behind him, and we wanted to get the energy of what they were doing, but they were singing so loud that at one point they had to move twelve feet away from the microphone, and we almost had to have them face the wall and sing completely away from the microphone in some parts, so we could get that sound to go into the groove without distorting. They kept the energy of the whole song going, and it was really great, but it was very challenging.

Scully lathe

Western Electric condenser microphone

ALLISON: It was like a theatrical production—Bernard designed different lighting for each session to give it a different feel, and he would rehearse with our house band before the performers arrived, and rehearse the camera crew with all the dolly moves so they would know when the lead vocalist would be singing; then it would go into a chorus, then the guitar or the banjo. There was a huge amount of preparation, because it was not just the music that had to be captured in one three-minute take—we had to capture the whole experience on film, and make it look natural, and do it smoothly enough that we didn't interfere with the performers.

It's a miracle that more things didn't go wrong. We had only two occasions when something broke. One was during the session with Los Lobos: the lathe works sort of like a clock, with this immense weight that you crank up, and then it slowly descends to the floor, and when it reaches the floor, the lathe stops and the recording is finished. During the Los Lobos session, the belt snapped and the weight came crashing down, almost on Nick's foot. Fortunately, Jack saved the day—he used to work with upholstery, so he drove around the corner to an auto upholstery shop, asked to use their sewing machine, and fixed the belt himself. We were all waiting on tenterhooks, wondering if he'd be able to do it, and he did, and then Los Lobos gave an incredible performance.

Control room door; recording session in progress

BERNARD: A project like this really has to be done as a team: you are working with a whole group of people and it's like you're in a trireme, you all have to row together. It's an exhilarating experience, but when I look at all the organization involved—finding a location, getting the performers together, keeping the equipment in order, rehearsing everybody, and coordinating the recordings—and then you think that in the 1920s they went on the road and did that month in, month out; they were in one location for a week in February, somewhere else in March, then they went out again in May. . . .

Just the problem of getting all the performers together: you might say, well, it's pretty difficult getting Willie Nelson, Merle Haggard, a Hawaiian troupe, a group of Cajuns from Louisiana, Alabama Shakes, and so on, and fitting that around the schedule of someone like Jack White—but imagine doing that in rural America in the 1920s. Now at least most people have telephones, but just think about having to get all these artists—and good ones—to come to somewhere like Johnson City on the fourth of April, and arranging all their lodging, their food—it's incredible.

One thing this taught me is that you can only truly appreciate history, and understand why things were done the way they were done, by actually going out and doing them yourself. You can glean a lot of knowledge from reading books or looking at some professor's theory, but there is no substitute for actually physically having the experience. It's like a boxer reading all the books about boxing and watching films of George Foreman and Joe Frazier, and studying what Jack Johnson did in particular situations. All of that may be helpful, but it's a world of difference from getting in the ring with a total stranger and having to apply that knowledge.

NICK BERGH: There are a number of things that were developed along the way out of necessity, like the buzzer and light system. That's always referred to [in descriptions of early record sessions], but I was hoping I could get away without them. But you can't have a bunch of dead wax before the musicians start playing—it's got to be, like, boom-boom; you have to know how quickly they're going to start, how quickly you're going to drop the stylus. So you realize, "Oh, we need a buzzer, we need start and stop lights—it's not for show, I have to have them, right now."

BERNARD: It was an amazing experience, and all of the performers seemed to share the sense that this was something special. For the final session, Willie Nelson and Merle Haggard arrived in a pair of giant tour buses—one silver, the other gold—and these twin vehicles just stood outside the studio, motionless, for almost half an hour, like the spacecraft in

"Recording here is kinda like back when you were at home doing it. Like it was when we were kids."
—Merle Haggard, recording with Willie Nelson

Lost Bayou Ramblers

Jack White

Pokey LaFarge

"It's more amazing than any digital, fancy-ass computer that I've ever seen, because it's actually moving parts, and you can see how it all works. . . . You feel like your soul is coming out of the speaker."
—Rhiannon Giddens

"The most exciting thing for me is that Louis Armstrong recorded on this. I just like the idea of everybody gathering around a microphone and just going. It's definitely an avenue to purity." —Seth Avett

Alabama Shakes

The Day the Earth Stood Still. Then these two figures in black emerged and strolled into the studio together, and they were clearly delighted to be confronted with the machine that their heroes, people like Jimmie Rodgers and Emmett Miller, used to record. They had composed a song especially for the session, "The Only Man Wilder Than Me," a kind of autobiographical ballad that seemed to bring the sessions full circle—these two legendary musicians, looking back to their own youth and the music that inspired them, and creating something new that connected them to that history.

NAS: This process, it's like you hear old records and you hear the way they sound, and you can picture how it must have been back then; you can kind of hear a different world. So recording here, it gave me a chance to go through a time machine, it brought me back to that world. This gives me a greater perspective, because it shows me that it's not because of something that started just thirty, forty years ago—it's something that's been going on before my parents were born, this music game.

Today it's like everything is so lit up, everyone's an automatic star. Back then you'd barely see a picture of these artists—we have it good now, it's amazing now compared to then—but still, they had something sacred, they had something that we don't possess. It was just music, people expressing themselves with the sound at that time, and it had nothing to do with the video, it had nothing to do with anything but the song. It shows me there's so much more to do, there's so much further I can go, but now I know the beginnings; this gives me the roots of all of it.

JACK WHITE: What's interesting about this project is that you're stripping away the technology back to the 1920s, and you can see a modern artist recording in this style and see how similar it is. The technology that has changed over and over again has sort of altered people's view of the performance, but all of these things are tricks to get you to pay attention to the story. Your point is to try to get someone drawn in, so you're using whatever tricks you can to make them do that—you're using melody, you're using rhythm, you're using the format it comes on, using the packaging and the photographs that come along with that, or a music video or whatever it is; those are all tricks to get everyone back to that story that's contained inside the song. And when you strip the technology away, you can see how similar people really are, how similar a pop artist now is to someone who was a pop artist in the 1920s. It's just our own individual styles that make us different.

Creators: Duke Erikson, Allison McGourty, and Bernard MacMahon

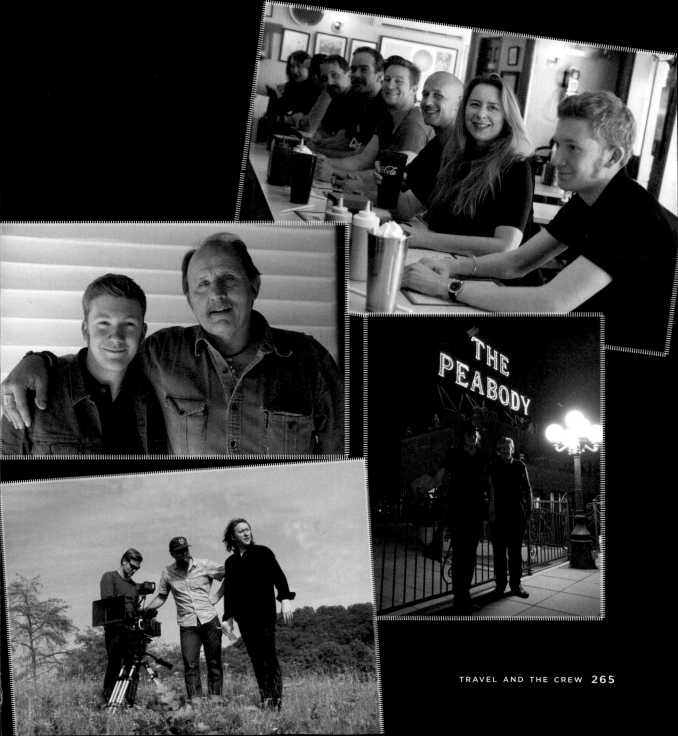

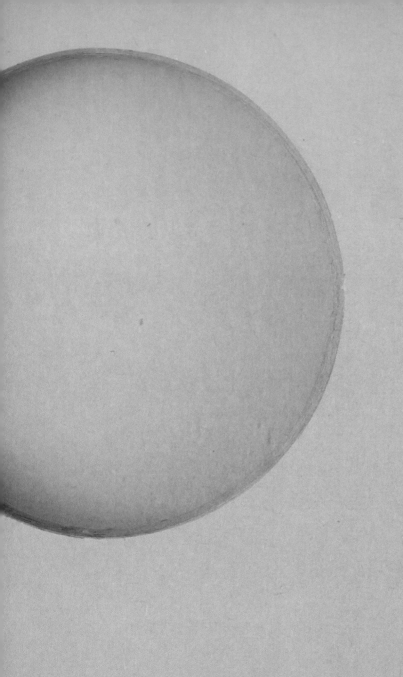

ACKNOWLEDGMENTS

* *

WE WOULD LIKE TO THANK

THE EXECUTIVE PRODUCERS
T Bone Burnett, Robert Redford, and Jack White.

THE *AMERICAN EPIC* TEAM
Nicholas Bergh, Adam Block, Sherwin Dunner, Duke Erikson, Patrick Ferris, Dan Gitlin, Peter Henderson, Bill Holderman, Larry Jenkins, Michael Kieffer, Jack McLean, Ian Montone, Nas, Jeff Rosen, John Tefteller, Elijah Wald, and Anthony Wall.

OUR CONSULTANTS AND ARCHIVISTS
Paul Alexander, Dave Anderson, Gary Atkinson, Scott Barretta, Bruce Bastin, Bill Pete Bergeron, Bill Brewington, Michael Brooks, Sheila Bumgarner, Joe Bussard, Garth Cartwright, John Cohen, Larry Cohn, Kathy Conkwright, Joy Conley, Les Cook, Harry Coster, John Eck, Lars Edegran, Kevin S. Fontenot, Mia Greendove, Todd Harvey, Len Horowitz, Jaime Jaramillo, Brad Kay, Don Kent, Miles Krueger, Steve Lasker, Joe Lauro, Rick Lepore, Mary Makley, Murray Lerner, Frank Mare, Barry Mazor, Robert "Mack" McCormick, Gilda Miros, Roger Misiewicz, Richard Nevins, Paul Oliver, Bengt Olsson, Clive Osborn, Frances Robb, Kinney Rorrer, Tony Russell, Ann Savoy, Stewart Schlosberg, Mike Seeger, Steve Sheldon, Russell Shor, Dick Spottswood, Karl Steig, Chris Strachwitz, Phyllis and Ken Swerilas, Paul Swinton, Tom Tierney, Professor Steve Tracy, John Troutman, Paul Vernon, Gayle Dean Wardlow, John R. Wheat, Daniel Wheeler, Pete Whelan, Charles K. Wolfe, Marshall Wyatt, and Kenneth Zoll.

OUR FRIENDS AND SUPPORTERS
Diane Aldred, Gavin Aldred, Erika Alfredson, Doug Allsopp, Chris Ancliff, Jason Anderson, Shari Annes, Martha Arenas, Gil Aronow, Jeff Bakken, Dave Ball, Tony Barrell, Mark Bashore, Richard Becker, John and Serena Benedict, Steve Berkowitz, Joe Berlinger, Mark and Carolyn Blackburn, Ben Blackwell, Anne and Jerome Boisard, Joe Boyd, John Boyd, Marea Boylan, Beth Brann, Gretchen Brennison, Paul Brown, Stuart Brown, Maik Brüggemeyer, Lt. Col. Gloria Bullock, Susan Buser, Mike Carey, Terry Carlson, Maggi Caridi, Robert Christgau, E.J. Cody, Chip Commins, Adrienne Connors, Tom Cording, William D. Coughlin, Vicki Cruz, Jean Cummins, Seth Daggett, Ben Dalby, Tom Davy, Roxy Erikson, Mark Ettinger, Ronald

and Vera Farrants, Gary Ferris, Alessandra Fremura, David Gahr, Geoff Gans, Garbage, Camilla Gibbs, Elizabeth Giles, Jenn and Asher Gitlin, Roger Glenn, Peter Golub, Gary Gonzales, Lonnie Goodwin, Ray Goto, Davis Guggenheim, Rachel Gutek, Gordon and Kathy Hamilton, John Harrington, Boyd Harvey, Alex and Lesley Hill, Gil Hopkins, Joanna Hughes, Prince Albert Hunt, Jim Hunt, Gail and Miller Ingram, John Jackson, David Jaymes, Marisa Jeffries, Jennifer and Peter Jesperson, Bob Johnson, Matthew Kelly, Heather Kenmure, Jennifer Kirell, Callie Khouri, Gayle and Scott Lane, Marion Koltai-Levine, George Kupczak, Taylor Lang, Guy Lavallée, Ken Levine, Richard Liebowitz, Barbara Ligeti, Pat MacMahon, Lalo Madina, Lana Mann, Carol Lusk, Frances McCain, Adrian McCusker, Gordon McGourty, Austin McLean, Tom Mullen, Nicholas Naro, Neil O'Brien, Alex Ogilvie, Dan Owen, Jim Parham, Elizabeth and Ralph Peer II, Paul Pieper, John Polito, Verna Polutan, Lisa Remington, David Rezak, Rod Randolph Richardson, Jarom Rowland, Andrew Ross, Melissa Ruella, Dr. John W. Rumble, Rob Santos, Jeffrey Schulberg, Jerry, Helen, Chris and Aileen Scully, Gudrun Shea, Timothy Shepard, Erin Simms, Benjamin Singleton, Eli Smith, Sarah Spruill, Bill and Jane Stetson, Richard Story, Nina Streich, Ben Swank, Bill Tapia, Joel Tefteller, Susie Tefteller, Lisa Verrico, Linh Vuong, Andrew Walker, Chris Walter, David Weiswasser, Mark Williams, Linda Wolfe, Geoff Wonfor, Doug Wong, Arash Zandi, and Nancy Zoll.

THE ORGANIZATIONS THAT HAVE HELPED US

Apollo Masters, AT&T, Audio Mechanics, BBC Arena, CEDAR Audio Ltd., Colorlab, City National Bank, Columbia Records, DGA, Edit Source, EMI Archive Trust, the George H. Buck Jr. Jazz Foundation, the Grace Richardson Fund, Hopi Cultural Preservation Office, iZotope, Lamm Industries, Legacy Recordings, LD Communications, the Library of Congress, MAC Cosmetics, MAC Presents, the Maritime Hotel, Media Insurance Brokers Ltd., the Memphis Police Department, Mercedes-Benz, Metropolis, the Mississippi John Hurt Foundation, Moving Image Research Collections at the University of South Carolina, Network Typing, the New York Public Library, OCL Studios, Park City Live, Pavek Museum of Broadcasting, Peermusic, [PIAS], Platinum Rye, Preferred Travel, ProQuest, Rainbo Records, Red Light Management, Sonic Studio, Sony Music, Squarespace, Sundance Institute, Sundance Film Festival, Syracuse University Bandier Program, Third Man Records, 2 Brydges Place, Verde Valley Archaeology Center, Wildwood Enterprises, and WGAW.

THE MANAGERS AND EXECUTIVES

Johnny Barbis, Colin Campbell, Stacey Fass, Michael Franks, Andrew Friedman, Gerry A. Fojo, John Grady, Rayburn W. Green, Wendy Hopkins, Marc Joachin, George Khangis, Kevin Kiley, Ken Levitan, Bonnie Levetin, Emily Lichter, Jackie Lopez, Michael Meisel, Kevin Morris, Henri Musselwhite, Dolphus Ramseur, Elliot Roberts, Mark Rothbaum, Anthony Saleh, Colin Smith, Damien Smith, John Smith, Christine Stauder, Randi Tolbert, Barry Tyerman, and Julian Wright.

THE FILM CONTRIBUTORS

Alyssabeth Archambault, John Ballard, Ted Bradley, Gary Breaux, Della Breaux Hook, Jeanie Broussard Breaux, Jimmy Breaux, Pat Breaux, Michael Brooks, Bob Burch, Kenny and Tracy Cannon, Larry Carver, John Carter Cash, Pastor Donnie Chapman, Annie Cook, Francis Duke, Honeyboy Edwards, Wade Falcon, Timothy Ferris, Antoine Carroll Fruge, Evans Fuller, Effie Gaspard, Ernest Gillespie, Allen Hebert,

Gwendolyn Hendon, Ann Hernandez-McKinney, Fernando Hernandez, Roger Hernandez, Mary Francis Hurt, Homesick James, Eugene Justice, Dale Jett, Jacqueline Knaff, Leigh Kuwanwisiwma, Bill Lester, Robert Lockwood Jr., Auntie Ka'iwa Meyer, Flo Millard, Jerry Mouton, Charlie Musselwhite, Hubert Nelson Jr., August Odom, Cyril Pahinui, Craig Raguse, Fern Salyer, Greg Sardhina, E.J. Satala, Anne Savoy, Ernestine Smith, Ken and Phyllis Swerilas, Bill Williamson and family, and Ken Zoll.

THE *AMERICAN EPIC* SESSIONS MUSICIANS
Alabama Shakes, The Americans, Peter Asher, the Avett Brothers, Carla Azar, Beck, Jay Bellerose, Edie Brickell, Chloe Feoranzo, Dominic Davis, Alison Elble, Frank Fairfield, Dean Fertita, Dom Flemons, Ana Gabriel, Rhiannon Giddens, Merle Haggard, Bobby Ingano, Hubby Jenkins, Elton John, Daru Jones, Fats Kaplin, Auntie Geri Kuhia, Pokey Lafarge, Lake Street Dive, Bettye Lavette, Los Lobos, Lost Bayou Ramblers, Taj Mahal, Roger Manning, Steve Martin, Fred Martin and the Levite Camp, Ashley Monroe, Nas, Willie Nelson, J. Micah Nelson, Alfredo Ortiz, Charlie Kaleo Oyama, Van Dyke Parks, Jerron Paxton, Christine Pizzuti, Lillie Mae Rische, Omar Rodriguez, Roberto Roffiel, Raphael Saadiq, Joshua Smith, Fred Sokolow, Stephen Stills, Bernie Taupin, Jack White, and Gabe Witcher.

OUR PROFESSIONAL ADVISERS
Ken Kraus at Loeb & Loeb LLP, Victoria Gaskill at Olswang LLP, Chris Perez at Donaldson + Callif, Michael Perlstein and Michael Martins at Fischbach, Perlstein, Lieberman & Almond, Alexis Grower at Magrath LLP, LeeAnn Hard and Steve MacNicoll at H2 Management, Andrea Richards and Tad Bieniek at Accounts Navigator, and Tim Sharman at MGR.

OUR PUBLISHERS, AGENTS, AND DESIGNERS
Matthew Benjamin at Simon & Schuster, Thomas Flannery and David Vigliano at AGI-Vigliano Literary LLC, Lorie Pagnozzi, Nat Strimpopulos at Third Man, and Brian Loucks at CAA.

OUR VERY SPECIAL THANKS TO

Ann Ray Charitable Trust, Jody and John Arnold, Katherine Chowdhary, Richard Constant, Jennifer and Bud Gruenberg, Tom and Marina McGourty, Ian and Pauline McLean, Pacific Islanders in Communications, Carrie Rhodes, Laura and Robert Sillerman, Peter Stampfel, Ann Tennenbaum and Thomas H. Lee, Peter Thompson, Jonathan Turner, the V&L Marx Foundation, Rosalind P. Walter, and Betsy Wolheim.

THIS BOOK IS DEDICATED TO THE MEMORY OF

Gladys Baudhuin, Alasdair Black, Eustis Firmin, Merle Haggard, Donna Kail, Tom McGourty, and Grant McLennan.

WE WILL NEVER FORGET THEM.

SOURCES

NOTE: *Quotations have been edited for flow and clarity, and questions and comments by interviewers have been eliminated. Nothing has been added, but in some instances phrases have been excised or reordered without ellipses, and when someone told the same story or addressed the same theme in more than one interview, versions have at times been combined to make a single, cohesive narrative. The aim throughout was to provide a readable, engaging, and accurate sense of the speech and opinions of the people being quoted, but scholars seeking phonographically exact quotations should consult the original sources, provided below.*

CHAPTER 1: THE FIRST TIME AMERICA HEARD HERSELF

Art Satherley, interview by Norm Cohen, Eugene Earle, and Ken Griffis, 1970. John Edwards Memorial Foundation Records (20001), Southern Folklife Collection, Wilson Library, University of North Carolina at Chapel Hill.

Ralph Peer, interview by Lillian Borgeson, 1958. John Edwards Memorial Foundation Records (20001), Southern Folklife Collection, Wilson Library, University of North Carolina at Chapel Hill.

Frank Walker, interview by Mike Seeger, 1962. Mike Seeger Collection (20009), Southern Folklife Collection, Wilson Library, University of North Carolina at Chapel Hill.

Maybelle Carter, interview by Ed Kahn and Archie Green, 1961. Archie Green Papers (20002), Southern Folklife Collection, Wilson Library, University of North Carolina at Chapel Hill.

CHAPTER 2: I'LL GET A BREAK SOMEDAY: WILL SHADE AND THE MEMPHIS JUG BAND

Will Shade interview by Paul Oliver, 1960. Courtesy of Paul Oliver.

Will Shade interview by Don Hill and David Maguin, 1961. Courtesy of the Donald R. Hill & David Mangurian collection, AFC 2007/018, American Folklife Center, Library of Congress, Washington, D.C.

Charlie Musselwhite interviews for *American Epic*, 2015.

CHAPTER 3: IN THE SHADOW OF CLINCH MOUNTAIN: THE CARTER FAMILY

Sara Carter (Bayes) and Coy Bayes, interviews by Ed Kahn, 1961–78. Ed Kahn Collection (20360), Southern Folklife Collection, Wilson Library, University of North Carolina at Chapel Hill.

Maybelle Carter, interview by Ed Kahn and Archie Green, 1961. Archie Green Papers (20002), Southern Folklife Collection, Wilson Library, University of North Carolina at Chapel Hill.

Ralph Peer, interview by Lillian Borgeson, 1958. John Edwards Memorial Foundation Records (20001), Southern Folklife Collection, Wilson Library, University of North Carolina at Chapel Hill.

Dale Jett and Fern Salyer interviews for *American Epic*, 2015.

CHAPTER 4: MY HEART KEEPS SINGING: ELDER J. E. BURCH

Ted Bradley and Ernest Gillespie interviews for *American Epic*, 2010–11 and 2015.

CHAPTER 5: GONNA DIE WITH MY HAMMER IN MY HAND: DICK JUSTICE AND THE WILLIAMSON BROTHERS

Ernestine Justice Smith, Eugene Justice, and Bill Williamson interviews for *American Epic*, 2004–6 and 2015.

CHAPTER 6: DOWN THE DIRT ROAD: CHARLEY PATTON AND THE MISSISSIPPI DELTA BLUES

H. C. Speir, interview by Gayle Dean Wardlow, 1970. From the Gayle Dean Wardlow Collection, Center for Popular Music, Middle Tennessee State University.

Honeyboy Edwards, Homesick James, Robert Lockwood interviews for *American Epic*, 2006.

Tracy and Kenny Cannon, interviews for *American Epic*, 2015.

CHAPTER 7: CHANT OF THE SNAKE DANCE: THE HOPI INDIAN CHANTERS

Leigh Kuwanwisiwma and E. J. Satala interviews for *American Epic*, 2015.

M. W. Billingsley film footage, 1956. Courtesy of Verde Valley Archaeology Center.

CHAPTER **8**: BIRD OF PARADISE: JOSEPH KEKUKU

Alyssa Beth Archambault and Kaʻiwa Meyer interviews for *American Epic*, 2015.

CHAPTER **9**: *MAL HOMBRE*: LYDIA MENDOZA

Ann Hernandez-McKinney and Roger Hernandez interviews for *American Epic*, 2015.

CHAPTER **10**: *ALLONS À LAFAYETTE*: THE BREAUX FAMILY

Frank Walker, interview by Mike Seeger, 1962. Mike Seeger Collection (20009), Southern Folklife Collection, Wilson Library, University of North Carolina at Chapel Hill.

Joe Falcon, interview by Chris Strachwitz, 1962, courtesy of the Arhoolie Foundation, archived at http://arhoolie.org/joe-falcon -interview.

Joe Falcon, interview by Lauren Post, 1965. Courtesy of Lauren Chester Post Papers, Mss. 2854, Louisiana and Lower Mississippi Valley Collections, Louisiana State University Libraries, Baton Rouge, L.A.

Jerry Mouton, Louis Michot, and Pat, Jimmy, and Gary Breaux interviews for *American Epic*, 2015.

CHAPTER **11**: AVALON BLUES: MISSISSIPPI JOHN HURT

Mississippi John Hurt, interview by Joe Hickerson, July 15 and 23, 1963, Library of Congress, Washington, D.C.

Mississippi John Hurt, interview by Pete Seeger, 1964, issued on *Mississippi John Hurt: Memorial Anthology*, Genes CD 9906/7, 1993.

Mississippi John Hurt, interview by George W. Kay, *Jazz Journal* 17, no. 2 (February 1964), pp. 24–26.

Bob Stephens interview by Michael Brooks, 1970. Courtesy of Michael Brooks.

Mary Frances Hurt and Dick Spottswood interviews for *American Epic*, 2015.

CHAPTER **12**: THE *AMERICAN EPIC* SESSIONS

Nick Bergh, Jack White, Ana Gabriel, and Nas interviews for *American Epic*, 2015.

PHOTO CREDITS

PRODUCTION PHOTOGRAPHER

Allison McGourty

ARCHIVAL PHOTO RESTORATION

Douglas Anderson, Dan Gitlin, Bernard MacMahon, and Roger Robles

ALL IMAGES © MAIDA VALE MUSIC LTD EXCEPT:

Peer Family Archives: 13; **Lebrecht Music & Arts Photo Library:** 14; **San Antonio Express-News/ ZUMAPRESS.com:** 16–17, 180–181, 182; © **International Center of Photography/Magnum Photos:** 31, 34–35, 45 (top) (Robert Capa); **Blues Images:** 36 (left), 37 (bottom), 117 (from the collection of John Tefteller and Blues Images); **Richard Nevins:** 36 (right); **Charlie Musselwhite:** 38, 54; **George Mitchell:** 39 (left), 40, 41, 42–43; **Courtesy of Demont Photo Management:** 48, 50 (William Claxton); **Memphis and Shelby County Room, Memphis Public Library:** 51; **Carter Family Museum:** 61; **Dale Jett:** 77; **Jacqueline Knaff:** 79, 86, 88 (right), 89, 93, 96, 99 (top); **Sony Music:** 82; **Ted Bradley:** 88 (left); **Ernest Gillespie:** 91; **Williamson Family:** 101, 104, 108, 110; **Justice Family:** 113; **Dockery Foundation:** 120, 121 (top); **Courtesy of Cary Ginnell:** 134; **Winslow Historical Society:** 135 (Courtesy of the Old Trails Museum); **Billingsley Photo Archive:** 145; **University of Iowa:** 151, 166; **AlyssaBeth Archambault:** 154–155 (right, bottom); **Victoria and Albert Museum, London:** 158–159; **Courtesy of National Archives at College Park, MD:** 165; **Arhoolie Foundation:** 169, 170, 173, 175, 178, 184, 185; **Hernandez Family:** 171, 172, 176, 186; **Wade Falcon:** 189, 190, 193, 205; **Jerry Mouton:** 194, 197, 200, 206–207, 211, 212, 213; **University of Louisiana at Lafayette, Center For Louisiana Studies:** 195, 198–199, 207 (Special Collections, Barnett Studio Collection); **Louisiana and Lower Mississippi Valley Collections, Louisiana State University Libraries, Baton Rouge, LA:** 206 (Courtesy of the Lauren Chester Post Papers, MSS 2854); **Getty Images:** 215, 216, 227 (top), 229; **Mississippi John Hurt Museum Foundation:** 218, 221, 230; **Memphis Library Special Collections:** 223.